Your economy

DAVID HOWELL warns that your overdraft will get bigger, and your bank manager will get less and less friendly about the whole thing. In fact, as long as the Government can squeez▮ the customer without discouraging heavy industry from keeping up a high rate of investment in new methods and equipment, it will continue to do so. Even when exports pick up again in the spring after their setback, the aim will be—or should be—to encourage activity in the investment industries and make them export more, at the expense of the consumer industries and imports.
Your tax payments will continue to be taken off you in an excruciatingly painful way, guaranteed to provide the minimum incentive to work hard and the maximum incentive to spend most of your office hours thinking of ways of getting round the tax laws. Schemes for radical tax reform will be two-a-penny and there will be talk of a move towards more indirect taxes—i.e., taxes on what you spend rather than on what you e▮▮▮▮
Your Amer▮▮▮ friends in the flat downstairs will spend hours trying to explain how their motherland manages to combine a balance of payments crisis with being by far the richest country in the world. There will be much talk about the need for the countries of the West to get together and solve their monetary problems. Schemes thought up by Keynes twenty years ago will be resurrected and a new spirit urged. The Government will examine possibilities—in co-operation with other governments, once they, too, agree to examine possibilities.
Your wages, *if* you belong to a strong union, will go on rising whether the economy booms, recedes, pauses for breath or just has a rolling readjustment. There will be renewed cries for a national wages policy. Our national economic objective will be—. or ought to be—to keep the whole complex rapidly expanding to provide more *output per man* and thus keep costs down and exports competitive while wages rise. If we fail to grow as fast as our neighbours and export rivals, then we will be condemning ourselves to permanently re-occuring bouts of inflation, balance of payments crises, Government restrictions and squeals from those restricted, in dreary and familiar sequence. Everyone will continue to talk about the need to re-orientate the economy towards growth.
Your pension contributions will go up on April 1st, as will State pensions themselves, from 50s. to 57s. 6d., unless you can get fixed up with some private scheme in your

firm. Otherwise, you will become involved in the most pie-eyed pensions system of graduated contributions ever to get on the statute book. The social services as a whole will go on costing more, and there will be talk of schemes for letting more people pay for their own services (education, health, etc.) or at least contributing.

ALAN DAY, editor of the National Institute's *Economic Review*, says that British economy is likely to be stagnant for the next year. The depression will not be world-wide, although it is likely that the United States will have a slight economic depression at the beginning of the year, too. In this country it will mainly affect consumer goods and will affect capital goods slightly. Unemployment may increase, and so may short-time working.

JO GRIMOND, M.P., agrees that we are going to see a slump in 1961, but it will not be a deep one. The scientists will pull us through, because techniques are improving all the time. We should overhaul the tax system to give an incentive to people to work harder: to start surtax at £2,000 is unrealistic. We should become more international to broaden our markets: the first step should be to join the Common Market immediately.

HAROLD WILSON, M.P., predicts that Britain's economic difficulties will come to a head in 1961. Economic expansion has been at a standstill for the best part of a year, unemployment and short-time working are spreading, our exports are falling further and further behind our still swollen imports. To deal with the fear of depression at home, the Government should be ending the credit squeeze and progressively bringing the bank rate down to a reasonable level.
What he would like to see is a more daring and venturesome economic policy—Bank Rate lowered to 4 per cent, as first step, direct aid to capital goods exports, tax and other incentives to encourage capital investment and modernisation in British industries. Should this look like expanding the demand for plant and machinery beyond the economic capacity of the country, then the Government should use building licensing and other controls to cut out the frills and speculative excesses, so that as a nation we can concentrate on the developments which will strengthen our production and trade.

NICHOLAS KALDOR, lecturer in economics at King's College, Cambridge, warns that 1961 is going to be a difficult year. Our balance of payments has been deteriorating very rapidly, and there seems to be nothing

to stop this being reversed. This has happened because exports have gone badly in the world markets, and our share of total exports has been falling. The actual level of our visible exports has been hidden by the inflow of American dollars into the country. And if this stops we shall see the real position of our exports.

Your films

FRANCIS WYNDHAM forecasts that Jean-Paul Belmondo will take over where Brando and Dean left off; that Peter Sellers will play Hamlet; that Visconti's *Rocco* will finally get a commercial showing, slightly cut, and run for ages; that *Cleopatra* will be a bore; that both Lawrence of Arabia films will open in the same week; that we shall be inundated by "sincere" films about homosexuality; that David Storey's *This Sporting Life*, directed by Karel Reisz, will be very good indeed; that during the year we shall see a film with *two* intervals; that films about the 'twenties will give way to films about the 'thirties; that *Lolita* will be surprisingly like the book.
Wishful Thinking Department: that there will be a slump in "adult" cowboy movies, Hammer horror films, Hollywood religious epics, Ingmar Bergman.

Your jewellery

MICHAEL GOSSCHALK predicts that it will be practical—for example: a clip that can be worn all day and still look good at night. More young people will buy jewellery and be more demanding about quality, workmanship and design. Engaged girls will at last be able to escape the three-stone diamond engagement ring. Rubies will be out of fashion. Diamonds, sapphires,

A century

of social conflict

as reflected in

The Queen

The Frontiers of Privilege

Quentin Crewe

Art Editor: Charles Rosner

Collins St James's Place

*We would like to thank all those who helped
with the research and the production of this book with advice
and with actual work. In particular we are grateful
to Miss Katharine Sachs, Miss Judy Innes, Mr Auberon Waugh
and Mr Terence Griffin, for their help in sifting
the vast quantity of material, and to
Mr Marcel Dauphinais for contributing layout and typography.*

All the material in this book has been taken from
The Queen *and we would also like to thank all these contributors,
writers, photographers and illustrators
whose work we have reproduced and Charles Rosner without
whom this book would not have been possible.*

J.S.

Designed and produced by CHARLES ROSNER & ASSOCIATES LTD LONDON

Contents

The Frontiers of Privilege

No. 1.—SEPT. 7, 1861. PUBLISHING OFFICE: 248, STRAND, LONDON. SIXPENCE, With Two Supplements.

A hundred years ago The Queen *was launched on Victorian Society, permission having been granted by Queen Victoria for the use of the name. Described as a 'Ladies Newspaper and Court Chronicle' it was aimed at those people who naturally attended Court functions, and those who would have loved to have been invited. The first proprietor was Samuel Beeton, the husband of the famous Mrs Beeton. He was not the kind of man to have much of an entrée to Court circles but despite the fact that he was forced to depend to a large extent on gleanings from his smarter friends, the magazine was incredibly well informed about the minutiae of Court and Society activities, not only in this country but abroad. Fashion also played a predominant part in the magazine. Since 1861* The Queen *has passed through the hands of at least half a dozen proprietors and many more editors. However, there has never been any doubt at which people* The Queen *has been directed, and it is solely their interests and attitudes, as interpreted by the different editors, that you will find reflected in this book. Thus it is not in any way a comprehensive history of the last hundred years. For instance the General Strike was never mentioned in* The Queen, *the editor at the time presumably considering it of no particular interest to his readers. All the material in this book is taken directly from the pages of* The Queen. *You may find it hard to believe some of the attitudes expressed. But remember that these are the immediate*

reactions of a relatively sheltered and most privileged section of the population at a moment in time. Looking back, it is this spontaneity which gives to the book its slightly bizarre quality—Hitler is praised for his kindness to animals, pneumatic tyres are dismissed as a passing fad, jazz is written off as a temporary craze.

'The Frontiers of Privilege' does not set out to point a moral, to be a social history or to evaluate the importance of the part played by the Upper Classes in the last hundred years. Its interest lies in the fact that the attitudes portrayed are completely prejudiced, utterly insufferable, entirely arrogant, totally self interested, shameless, and essentially British.

JOCELYN STEVENS Editor-in-Chief,
The Queen

The Victorians

Saturday, July 19, 1890.

No. 2273.—Vol. LXXXVIII.

Price Sixpence.

THE QUEEN

HONI SOIT QUI MAL Y PENSE

V.R.I

Subtle, fragrant, indescribable,
but all pervading is that lovely thing
we call good-breeding.

September 1861. For the rich, leisured women of England, it is not an eventful period. Indeed it is a dull one and promises to continue so. The social patterns of the country are deeply cut. So little happens to stimulate the imagination that small children sharing a bed take it in turns to sleep on the outside, 'lest Boney should come in the night'. Nothing has happened to alarm since Napoleon, so he remains the only threat to titillate small minds with fear. And older minds know no fear. From the rock-like pinnacle of privilege the upper classes gaze into the future with well-bred, confident arrogance. Viewed from this height all is order and peace. An unchanging millennium stretches out ahead, safe, secure, rich.

It seems that nothing can chip at the fabric of society. Factory Acts, poor laws, a slightly broader franchise. What of them? They make no difference to the vast estates and to their owners. A very few other people appear to be richer than they ought to be. That is disquieting, but the distribution of wealth is only fractionally wider.

The way of life of the sort of women for whom *The Queen*—Ladies Newspaper and Court Chronicle—catered, was governed by an unchanging set of rules. The very hours at which they did things, what they should wear, where they should go—every detail was controlled by this code. The most striking aspect of the code was its absolute rigidity. The inexorable quality of the rules made it seem that society was as ordered as nature. It would take an act of God seriously to alter the social pattern. Conformity was the only passport

to success, to a state as it were of social grace. In an article on how to give a grand ball, if not acquainted with enough grand people, it was suggested that the hostess should get the most fashionable lady she knew to co-operate, allow her to draw up the invitation list without interference, and certainly not ask any dreary middle class friends out of duty. The woman intending to give such a party would realise that she was bound to lose some of her friends in this way, but the advice given was that she should not worry about this.

The daily life of these women was extremely circumscribed. They did not feel it was necessary or proper for them to concern themselves with anything which might be considered serious. On the other hand, they said that earnestness was a grand quality. And earnest they were about those things which came within their narrow scope.

'Of the Drawing Room itself we would say a few words . . . The crowning mischief, as we take it, is the way in which presentation at Court is now so vulgarised, that it has lost all value and meaning as a title to social distinction. Formerly, presentations were confined to the true aristocracy of the country, the peerage, the superior landed gentry, persons of distinction in art, science and letters and the holders of offices of dignity under the Crown . . . It is now no longer so. Presentations are now so vulgarised that literally ANYBODY who has sufficient amount of perseverance or self confidence may be presented. The wives of all Members of Parliament are presented

Court dress to be worn at the Queen's Drawing Room

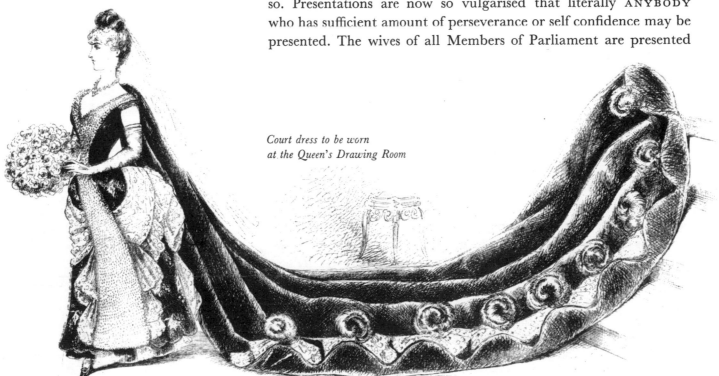

Wedding breakfast table (1870)

and they in turn present the wives and daughters of local squires, and other small magnates. There is no knowing where this is to stop . . . Those who have the ruling of these matters had better look to this matter and remedy the mischief in time, or they may be assured of it that the honour of being presented at Court will soon cease to be a mark of distinction at all.' The same complaint had been heard for five hundred years.

The trivialities of life had become invested with an importance which they could not possibly justify. Clothes, for instance: 'The Queen notices any irregularity in a moment, and it would be by no means pleasant to receive a reproof from the Lord Chamberlain, as I heard some gentleman did who appeared in levee dress at a Drawing Room.' It was even necessary to have a doctor's certificate if one were going to wear a low dress with safety at a Court Drawing Room.

The picture of the perfect woman emerges as one of the few things that varied a great deal over the sixty years. When *The Queen* was founded, women were still regarded as frail objects for the exercise of chivalry. In discussing railway accidents, what concerned the paper was that women might die in them. It did not seem to matter if men lost their lives too. In the 1870's, it was essential for a woman lunching alone in public to have an escort. 'Where can a lady who is shopping, or lives in the outskirts of London have lunch? St James's Hall, Verey's, Blanchard's and the principal railway stations, probably head the list . . . but . . . ladies are somewhat shy of entering

St James's Hall alone. Similarly, a male escort or the protection of members is much needed when lunching at Verey's and Blanchard's . . .' 'Rule's world-renowned oyster house in Maiden Lane, which notwithstanding its situation in a dingy back street behind the Adelphi, is perfectly respectable, and for the speciality it supplies, unrivalled. I have seen ladies lunching at Rule's, and congratulate them on their courage and discernment.'

Chaperones were essential for débutantes, and it was almost impossible for a man to accompany a single woman. 'In the case of a gentleman accompanying a young lady to the theatre as sole chaperon, he must be, of course, a near relative, either father, brother or uncle; but in no case would a friend be available for the purpose, however intimate he might be with her family, unless he were a very old gentleman indeed, and even this would be unconventional and inadvisable.'

By the end of the century, the attitude was changing. 'The girls of the day are fine girls, handsome girls, well grown and well developed; they have a splendid physique, they are strong and healthy and have good appetites and good digestions. They can dance into the small hours of the morning, night after night; they are good for any number of games of tennis; they can row a good stroke on the river, they can paddle a canoe, they can make up an eleven at cricket.' They were no longer regarded as fragile, and an advertisement for Scott's Emulsion reads: 'Healthy flesh means life, energy, health and power to overcome or withstand disease . . . We can have flesh by taking Scott's Emulsion. Not loose superficial flesh, but flesh that is solid and healthy. Thin angular women ought to have the flesh Scott's Emulsion supplies. It makes angles give way to curves of beauty.'

It was even suggested that women were becoming aware of matters which before had been quite unmentionable. 'As to Mrs. Bruce's sentimental twaddle regarding the glory and purity of the sex, it is rather out of place in these nineteenth century days when almost every girl as soon as she leaves the schoolroom—sometimes before—reads a daily paper (divorce and breach of promise cases included), Ouida's last novel and the leading magazines.'

It must not be thought, however, that they were yet considered as potential equals for men. The Warden of All Souls and the Warden of Wadham in 1889 spoke strongly against the introduction of women to the University—not only on mental but also on sanitary grounds.

Meet of the Four-in-Hand Club in Hyde Park (1885)

Although the picture of the perfect woman might change the picture of the imperfect one was always the same. The whipping boy of *The Queen* was the parvenu. 'The prejudice against parvenus — that is against those who have raised themselves from comparative poverty to affluence, and from insignificance to relative importance may be, and is, carried to an unjust and most injurious extent . . . Parvenus of both sexes are notorious for their insolence and tyranny to all servants and social inferiors. The intellectual pretensions of the parvenu are as colossal as his knowledge is small . . . A parvenu, out and out, is as selfish as he is pretentious, he is as dignified as he is ungrateful.' It is this question of how to behave, of which the parvenu was the hideous object lesson, which seems to have pre-occupied the mind of the Victorian reader. It was naturally the woman parvenue who was most suspect. In a leader on misalliances it was suggested that artists and self-made men were most likely to fall into this trap. If they married on the way up, 'they grow but the wife does not. Excellence in their art, their special science, brings with it social esteem and conventional approbation. They are adopted by their superiors in station and refinement, and the self-respect born of success soon fuses them into harmony with their better world. But they cannot drag their dead-weight with them. Ladies, even the most enthusiastic about atoms and the most frank in comradeship with artists, object to a woman who looks like a cook in her Sunday clothes, and who talks as she looks. It jars too much . . .'

'*Five o'clock tea
at the Royal Academy*'

ROYAL TIGER SLIPPER
Expressly Embroidered for
"THE QUEEN"

"A Good Catch."

"Well Blocked"

The first professional women cricketers (1890)

The attitudes of women confined by this strict social code were not likely to be liberal.

Servants were one of the primary concerns of the paper. None of the leaders on any other subject ever contained the venom and the strength of those devoted to this question. The tone of writing about them never altered from the first issue, which accused them of being more snobbish than their masters. There was really nothing good ever said about servants in the magazine. The nearest that it ever got, was a note which said that servants, both male and female, were, after all, but human beings and therefore subject to the vices of humanity. It is interesting that it was necessary to say both male and female, as though one sex might be human and not the other. But more interesting is that their humanity was discovered only by the fact that they gave away to the same temptations as their masters.

"A SLOW OVERHAND."

Badminton in the tropics

There was nothing that servants could do right. Why should cooks drink more than any other class of servant was a question often asked. 'There is no one practice so fraught with danger as that which is called the Sunday evening out. Unless the girl is positively known to spend the time in the company of respectable friends, the privilege ought never to be granted. Make such arrangements as will allow her to go to Church in the morning or afternoon but not in the evening, especially in short days.'

The attitude to servants raises the whole question of class consciousness, and the absolute certainty which upper class women had of their right to their position in society. Occasionally, some view would be aired, described as a prejudice, that the middle classes might be morally superior to the upper classes. This sort of thing could be conveniently squashed by cosy statistics: 'The moral to be culled from the state of business in the Divorce Court is that the old prejudice about the moral superiority of the middle classes over the upper is absolutely disproved and reversed . . . Directly the Bill became law, upwards of *two thousand* petitions were presented, proving that during the whole time which divorce had been an expensive luxury, the absence of such cases among the middle classes had been due not so much to the absence of cause but the inability or unwilling-

ness to incur heavy expense. The cheapening of Divorce has, however, effected an extraordinary relevation. The middle classes seem to be by no means as moral as they were supposed to be.'

A social conscience was a concept foreign to these Victorians—at least in the sense in which we understand it. There existed certainly the paternalism of a feudal society, a feeling of responsibility towards inferiors, untinged by guilt. The fact that some people were superior was an accepted and even a welcome fact. God, if anyone, was to blame for any seeming injustice and a proper awareness of God's impeccable judgement did not admit of any criticism of the system He had ordained.

'London is beyond compare the richest city in the world; does it not seem strange then that in the midst of so much riches a human being, the image of his Creator, should lie down on a doorstep to die of absolute want? On Monday night in the heart of the metropolis of the world—in the midst of riches such as no city of ancient or modern times ever yet contained—two of God's creatures died for want of a crust of bread! There is a gross wrong somewhere; in remembrance of Him who calls the poor His brothers let something be done that will prevent a recurrence in this, the boasted land of liberty.'

'Beauties of the present day'

No fault could be found, but on the other hand the poor and the unfortunate by their inevitable existence served the useful purpose of providing objects for the devout pity and generosity which it was the duty of the privileged classes to show. An admirable arrangement, which was used to the full. 'One capital error runs through most people's recipes for soup for the poor. What the poor like is a simple soup. I find they like a little spice in their food, probably it is easier for digestion than vegetables. Their stomachs weakened by a long period of the simplest and least nourishing food, will not digest anything very different from their usual fare. I think they might be taught to like lentil soup made without meat, thickened with good dripping and flavoured with a little onion or salt.'

The poor were there to be alternately bullied and watched over. No sentimentality was lavished upon them, the attitude toward them being governed by a strict practicality. The working class as a whole were regarded with gentle disapproval, coloured by a suspicion that they were extravagant and drunken. The poor were viewed with an active distaste except at Christmas time.

Suggestions that the poor were deserving were frequently questioned in articles and it was pointed out that 'poverty and misery, be it remembered, are more generally the results of vice, laziness and improvidence, than of misfortune'.

As we have seen, the parvenu was the object of gravest suspicion and was to be attacked not only for his own shortcomings in society, but also as a person who ruined the social structure below him.

'In the country, the British Workman likes and respects every squire and parson who is really worthy of affection and veneration. In mining and manufacturing districts there is, alas, a woeful strain on the relations between master and man. The founder of most large businesses has generally been placed by birth but little, if at all, above those under him in trade. The Englishman despite his demand for equal political rights is yet far more willing to serve under what he calls a real gentleman than under a successful member of his own class.'

As a summary of the attitude to the working class comes this extract which can be equated with the discovery that servants are after all human beings.

'The existence of the working classes as a separate, very distinguishable, very influential section of society is a comparatively recent invention . . . The fact is, that of working people as a class the middle and upper sections of society really know very little. Working men and

'An Australian Boudoir'
from a painting by A. J. Wall

women are to be met of course in daily life; but as they come generally on business, intercourse with them is mostly confined to what is absolutely necessary to be said and done, and there ends. Of the homes and manner of life of the working people, of their amusements, their modes of thought, their associations, how very little is really known to the people who are a step above them on the social scale . . . Such facts have been recently furnished with regard to the working classes in a book which has been written by a journeyman engineer. A careful perusal of the book—which is called *Some Habits and Customs of the Working Classes*—shows the reader that there is much to like and to appreciate among the working people, though their standards and customs may not be quite those of Mayfair; and, after all, one rises from it with the conviction that with the working classes, as with others, there is a great deal of human nature in the world.'

Whatever happened, the lower classes, and for that matter the middle classes, were to remain in their place. If they tried to venture out they would be savagely attacked. 'During the second half of the month of August, Boulogne is not a pleasant place for quiet English families. The Britannia snob is everywhere in force and seems to take the greatest possible pains to prove his descent from the ape—turn which way you will, you are brought into immediate and disagreeable contact with Cheapside and the Minories a-holiday-making. There is no reason why these people should not have their outing as well as their employers, but it is scarcely worth while to encounter them when flushed with the unusual possession of a ten-pound note.'

The hereditary principle was regarded as unshakable, but when it was necessary to do so, it was quite possible to find excuses for anyone. When Mr Tennyson became a peer a great deal of trouble was taken to prove that he was descended from Edward III, which must be true of many more people than the Upper Ten Thousand. *The Queen* also listed thirteen other English Kings as his ancestors, apparently not realising that if one is descended from one King one is likely to be descended from the previous ones as well.

In the same way that social relationships were divided and regulated with enormous care, so the women's attitudes to ideas were regimented and formalised. Religion as a subject was never mentioned in the magazine, presumably because everyone was assumed to be a believer, in spite of Darwin and in spite of Edmund Gosse. The only actual comments on religion are none-too-veiled attacks on Catholicism, in particular directed towards Italy; frequent mentions of the

'Interior of the dog hospital, Holloway. The animals portrayed from the life'

'*A Header at Boulogne*'

Bible as an improving book, especially for foreigners and colonial
subjects; and occasional mentions of fashionable preachers. There
was a healthy Protestant tang discernible from time to time. It was
reported with approval that a sculptor in Australia had been sent to
jail for two years and fined £100 for questioning the morality of some
parts of the Old Testament, and speaking disrespectfully of the personal character of Moses. The attitude to Catholicism was very
marked. It seems that they almost suspected that the Catholic
religion was promulgated without any reference to either Testament.
'It is with no sectarian view that we call attention to an event which
marks the onward progress of thought and the extended freedom of
mental activity in the Italian peninsula. We allude to the publication
in half-penny numbers so as to place it within the reach of all classes
—of a translation of the Bible. But a few years back, such a venture
would have been impracticable. In many states the Catholic authorities would have prohibited the publication by fine or imprisonment.
It is exceedingly gratifying to know that the Bible will supplant much
of the lewd and profane refuse with which the Italian populace is at
present almost exclusively supplied. The publication of the Bible in
a cheap form amongst a people to many of whom it has been a sealed
book marks a new era in the history of a nation.'

Their attitude to the Roman Church seems curiously violent in its
old-fashionedness, until one comes to compare it with the contemporary attitudes to progress, to foreign countries, to nature, to cruelty
and suffering. In all these things, the Victorians appear to have been
far closer to the attitudes of two hundred and fifty years before their
time than we are today to the Victorians themselves. Certainly, they
were closer to the earth than we are. The nature notes which
appeared with steady regularity throughout the century presumed
in the readers a knowledge of country lore which only a specialised
magazine would expect today.

With this closeness to nature went a certain callousness, almost a
streak of barbarity. There is the repeated fascination with accidents;
flogging is called wholesome. They can even run the risk of making a
joke of a succession of suicides from Waterloo Bridge: 'The contagion
spread rapidly and silly girls and wretched young women go there
daily to drown themselves. Shame on the authorities that they
should render such disgraceful exhibitions possible . . . . Here are
women, the very doves of creation, bounding before all the world into
the Thames and doing so at Waterloo Bridge as if there was the
proper place to depart in the most effective and fashionable manner.

THE FASHIONS

Expressly designed and executed in Paris for

"THE QUEEN"

An Illustrated Journal & Review.

6d. WEEKLY.

The Great Eastern
in Cork Harbour
after a storm

The Ladies' Saloon
during the storm

We must express the hope that at once a stop will be put to this mad and fatal tendency.'

While they are quite happy attacking the Italians, French, Spanish and Portuguese for cruelty to animals, they did not hesitate to suggest putting an asthmatic mouse in a draught to make it wheeze: 'Can you inform me whether singing mice are very uncommon? I lately heard one in my room and it made quite a flute-like musical noise, almost like the singing of a bird. (The so called singing in mice is really only an asthmatic wheezing, arising from an obstruction of the air passages. When captured the singing can always be produced at will by putting the cage in cold air—Ed.)'

By the 1880's, there is some suggestion of greater gentleness and it is interesting to note that by this time they were able, on rare occasions, to wonder whether all was well in England: 'The practice of infanticide which has long prevailed in the East is one which has

A pit disaster
'Bringing up the dead'

excited the horror and indignation of the English people, and every effort has been made in countries under English rule to put an end to it. In most cases, their efforts have been attended with success, and it is doubtful whether in any country under British Government infanticide prevails to as great an extent as it does in England itself.'

Running parallel with this ruthlessness is an almost superstitious ignorance. Progress was welcomed with great suspicion: 'In paraffin we appear to have taken to our bosoms an explosive viper . . . A commission is sitting to enquire into the effect of railway travelling upon public health. One of our leading clubs has recently voted gas out of its apartments, because it makes people go bald and poisons the air. The rapid dazzling motion of the dial pointers of the electric telegraph is damaging to the eyes . . .' 'The Medical journals have proved beyond dispute that excessive railway travelling has increased the necessity for lunatic asylums.' It is certainly true that we ask the same questions ourselves today, as to whether speed of life does not cause the neurosis from which we believe we suffer, but this view of the Turkish bath seems strangely wide-eyed: 'After about four months of the use of the Turkish bath in a lunatic asylum, seventeen persons have been cured and sent home to their friends. Thirty idiotic patients have been removed to a higher class and rendered capable of enjoyment. The introduction of Turkish baths into all public institutions is strongly recommended.'

In spite of the speed of land travel, abroad still seemed very far away, except inasmuch as the rich travelled on the Continent, and it is almost surprising to find in 1863 that it was possible for such naïve

Children of an orphan working school making up their mourning for the Prince Consort

INVENTORIES.

Women at Work.

FLORIST

IRISH SPINNER

WELSH SPINNER

A Turkish bath (1872)

*A diary of a lady's trip
through the tropics*

mistakes to be made in the magazine about Australia. One would suppose it to be a joke if the rest of the article were not absolutely serious. 'When it is midnight in Europe it is noon in Australia and reciprocally. When it is fine weather in Australia the barometer sinks—to announce bad weather it rises. The heat flows from the north, the cold from the south and it is on top of the mountains that the heat is greatest. Everywhere is the same contradiction. The bees do not sting, the birds do not sing; the owl comes forth during the day. The trees do not give any shadow because it is the edge of their leaves not the side which is turned towards the sun.'

Abroad is a hazardous place: 'There appears to be no doubt that no inconsiderable proportion of the girls who accept situations abroad, and, more especially in Belgium, are doomed to a life of infamy to which death itself would be far preferable.' Even America is not very reliable. 'The danger of ladies allowing themselves to become involved in matrimonial engagements with foreigners is very great . . . The marriage laws of other nations do not accord with our own. An American citizen marrying an English woman can get a divorce in many states of the Union on the slightest possible grounds, and as long as he remains in his own country he will then be not answerable for the support of his wife. The moral of all this is that, however romantic it may be to become engaged to an interesting foreigner the risk is great.'

But while foreigners were suspect, the notion of travel as an elegant pastime was very attractive to the Victorians. The magazine was filled with articles about Italy, Egypt and even the West Indies, as suggested places for, not holidays, but just journeying abroad. It was part of the necessary accomplishments of any fashionable person that she should have been abroad. Whether they actually enjoyed the travelling itself so much is rather doubtful, because there were many complaints about life abroad, the discomforts, the food, and of course the perpetual bogey of being assaulted: 'It was with a feeling of indignation too great for words that I read the following which appeared in several Paris newspapers: "Une Anglaise embrassée dans la rue". After hearing the facts of the case, that an English governess had been kissed in the streets by a workman against her will, the court proceeded to sentence the man to eight days' imprisonment. Several French newspapers have expressed sympathy for the poor workman. To the English, however, the subject is not one which can be passed over so lightly. Have the English girls who come to Paris always acted with the same prudence and self-respect as they

A LADY'S TRIP THROUGH THE TROPICS

would have done at home?' The judge had said during the case that *no* girl can be kissed against her will, even if only an English governess.

In the same way, it was essential to have some sort of interest in the arts. Rather as foreigners were despised, so were artists, unless they were really fashionable, like Millais or Lord Leighton. Their view of how artists lived was predictable: 'It is not a little surprising to be taken to some of the houses of the literary and semi-artistic families living in and near London. An atmosphere of mouldy decay pervades the house which is painted in dark green blues. The walls are hung with every conceivable absurdity—sconces where no candles are ever lighted, gongs which are not to sound . . . while dinner services of china are strung on the staircase . . . The poor girls try to dress in a way which they fondly believe to be artistic and end in looking like rag dolls. They tie the refuse of Cairo round their waists and wisps of strange fabrics round their necks. Peacocks' feathers eye us from unaccountable situations, and frills of old lace, so dirty as to be almost nasty, garnish throats that would look much better in clean linen collars . . . Tidy hair is inadmissible. It should give the impression that it is subject to being torn whenever its owner is carried away by the tumult of feeling produced by a passionate poem of Rossetti's, or the tragic ending of a three volume novel. It must never be fastened up securely, but must be ready to fall down at the slightest provocation. It must be free to the four winds of heaven and look like well tossed hay.'

Travelling cap

*The explorer Stanley
camping in a palm grove*

THE IDLER

ST JAMES'S THEATRE

Madame Melba

The Queen devoted always a certain amount of space to the theatre, to books and to painting. On the whole, they wanted the theatre to be as conventional as possible: 'It may be true, and undoubtedly is so, that the grossness of speech and action which in former times disfigured the stage would not now be permitted; even Shakespeare has to be expurgated. But that is only a part of the generally more decent external tone of society.'

The ballet was regarded as absurd. There were frequent attacks upon it. It was dismissed as being 'nothing but a means of exhibiting female figures for the benefit of certain sitters in the stalls and higher priced parts of the theatre. Modest women turn away their heads, and others gaze with a sort of petrified horror of attraction, wondering whether these sprawling creatures are indeed women with feeling like themselves.'

Private theatricals were very much in fashion, and it was a regular part of country house visiting to put on some sort of performance. 'It is very desirable that the date of a play should enable the performers to present themselves in costume of fancy dress; the change in attire gives confidence to the actors, and is always more picturesque than an every day dress.'

The paper's approach to painting was very much what one would expect. Rossetti, Holman Hunt, and Landseer were all admired. Whistler and the Impressionists were despised. When Rossetti painted *Dante's Dream on the Day of Death of Beatrice*, they wrote that he had completed a large and important painting in which the figures were not less than life size. The colour was magnificent, yet sombre, and the whole work was intensely pathetic, and wrought in the grandest style. It was said that few works by Englishmen approached it in noble qualities. When writing about *The Shadow of Death* by Holman Hunt, they said: 'Mr Hunt, true to his principles as leader among the Pre-Raphaelites, who some years ago sought to reform the errors into which the section of the British School of Art represented by Mr Etty, R.A. had fallen, has executed every portion of his picture with greatest fidelity and truth . . . In ability as a draughtsman, Mr Hunt yields to no one . . . the colouring of the whole work is as rich as it is harmonious and colourful.' And they were fond enough of Landseer to have wished for him to get a title: 'So great a favourite as he was with Royalty and the Upper Ten Thousand, had he cared to lay himself out for hereditary honours Landseer might easily have commanded a baronetcy.' They deeply mourned the death of Lord Leighton, quoting his last words as being:

Love to the Academy and its members. About Whistler, they became impassioned. It is noticeable that some of the strongest attitudes taken by *The Queen* are attacks on affairs which they did not understand at all: 'The Yacht Race—a symphony in B sharp by James Whistler, is really too ridiculous, and one is getting tired of the works this painter thinks proper to exhibit.' 'Now, to take the portrait of Mr Whistler's mother, arranged in grey and black. This is a life size portrait likeness, which was in the Royal Academy Exhibition of 1872. A venerable looking lady, there being considerable character in the head; but in effect the work is flat as a board, and possessed altogether of but little more art than is met with in the black profile portraits occasionally taken in the streets by itinerant artists.'

Royalty Theatre, Soho

HAND SCREEN IN BEAD WORK
Expressly designed for
"THE QUEEN"

When discussing Impressionism, the art critics were able to appreciate that Impressionism was not realism, but one seems strangely at variance with the facts when he concludes that Impressionist paintings have no atmosphere. 'One has no wish to speak unfairly of what may be the genuine beliefs of a body of artistic brethren, but we must say that professors of Impressionism appear to delight in form that is grotesque; colouring that has hitherto been accepted as a principle of harmony is ignored, and in many instances they certainly dispense with the idea of atmosphere altogether . . . We prefer not to pursue the subject further and leave the collection to its admirers.'

The book page of *The Queen* was curiously dull. It contained mostly short reviews of books, usually novelettes which have never since been heard of. They admired Dickens, Thackeray, Trollope in a rather unpersuasive way, but in the forty years of the Victorian period there was no one piece of literary criticism either surprising in its unexpectedness, or interesting for its perception. Only on the matter of Zola were they at all adventurous, in describing *L'Assomoire* as a nauseous and powerful novel, and nearly twenty years later, when Emile Zola visited England in 1893 they showed a tolerance of someone whom one would have expected them to abhor. 'When you shake hands with him, the softness and delicacy of his hand is as General Harrison's, the late President of the United States, or Mr Oscar Wilde's; they are not the kind of hands that run up long scores at cricket; Mr Zola may transgress our ideas of decency on the subject matter of his writings, but he is not immoral.' This is, perhaps, the more typically English attitude—he is not necessarily a dirty man because he writes a dirty book, whereas on the Continent he would inevitably be considered so.

'Fair Artistes'

'Amongst Trees and Flowers'

A newspaper of this sort, dedicated to women, naturally carried a great deal about interior decoration, and in this field *The Queen*, perhaps more confident of its opinions, was able to take a line both definite and humorous in protesting against useless and ugly trifles accumulated 'in order to take off the naked look of a room. What defect in the vision can induce any human being to cover a real, genuine red flower pot that is exactly what it pretends to be and nothing more nor less with spangled or parti coloured crimped paper? . . . Again, who is guilty of the folly which amounts to a crime of having been the inventor of little mats—of little mats that repose upon tables as resting-places usually for something only less worthy than themselves. They are abominable in everything, in wool, in beads, in silk, in painted velvet; yet parents pay for their daughters' learning to create these atrocities, among other branches of fancy needlework, at boarding schools . . . Why does nearly every middle class house in the country break out into a spring rash of antimacassars? They are not pretty in themselves and they inevitably destroy the possible prettiness of anything that may be beneath them.'

They are unexpectedly antagonistic to the fussier aspects of Victorian decoration, blaming as usual the middle and lower classes. Sometimes, however, they could lose their heads, and suggest 'a fountain in the centre of the table, or a huge block of ice on a crystal stand or tall branching palms that seem to grow out of the table . . . In a more modest way, palmetto plants in pots are extremely nice . . . A very tasteful and fanciful centrepiece made its appearance this season — a large sheet of looking glass, lying flat upon the table, with a margin of green velvet or narrow troughs, filled with flowers. Swans float on the surface of this, among water lilies, or cupids paddle their own canoe across, or drive a train of water fowl, harnessed to their triumphal car.'

'Cosy Corner
for a Gentleman's Room'

Given that these were the attitudes of the upper classes of Victorian England, it is not hard to understand that their way of life consisted really of nothing so much as an elaborate system of living, no more than that. The chief concern of the paper was to see that its readers were familiar with the latest trends of everyday social existence. The paper was almost a weekly book on etiquette. It gave instructions rather severely to its readers on all subjects, from chaperones to tipping. Again, in these parts of the magazine they were extremely forceful. They felt on safe ground and were quite determined to be arbiters of behaviour. The next few quotations illustrate the kind of worries which *The Queen* was prepared to assuage for its readers. Anyone reading the paper would be confident that she was able to set forth into Society without committing any of the solecisms which were the greatest dread of the time. It is noticeable that some of the remarks are by no means pusillanimous. *The Queen* was very seldom priggish, and in fact often encouraged its readers to abandon some convention which it thought exaggerated.

. . . 'The guests are sent in to dinner on the first evening according to their rank; but it has now become the fashion at many country house parties on the second succeeding evening of the visit, for the gentlemen to draw lots as to which of the ladies they should take in to dinner . . . A country house party generally resolves itself into two or more cliques as far as the ladies are concerned, as gentlemen as a rule are not much given to cliquing. In this manner and on the first evening as soon as the ladies have left the dining room for the drawing room, these little cliques are tacitly formed and continue unbroken until the close of the visit . . . The evening amusements . . . vary very much . . . Napoleon baccarat and roulette are now much played in society . . . At eleven o'clock the ladies usually retire to their rooms . . . Some hostesses prefer keeping late hours and sitting up until after twelve but these late hours for the ladies are not popular with the gentlemen as they are not supposed to retire to the smoking room until the ladies have left the drawing room and gentlemen invariably spend a couple of hours in that apartment before retiring to rest. Ladies are never expected to invade the privacy of the smoking room . . . Breakfast is rather a silent meal than not . . .'

'Ladies when invited to a country house are often in doubt as to the number and richness of the gowns it will be necessary to take with them, as at some houses and in some counties dress is carried to a far greater excess than in others; although where the hostess is a good dresser the invited guests would bear this in mind in selecting those

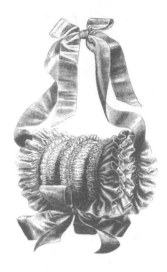

to be worn on the occasion, as a guest who is what is termed as dowdy—that is, a person who dresses without taste or style, and whose gowns have about them a faded and chiffoné appearance, finds but little favour in the eyes of a dressy hostess unless this consideration were outweighed or counterbalanced by either high rank, great wealth or some equally good equivalent . . .

'It is also often a matter of doubt for ladies as to whether they shall . . . wear the grandest evening dress they have brought with them on the first night of arrival or whether they shall reserve it for the second evening's wear; some prefer the former alternative with a view to making a good impression and looking their best on the first night of the visit; while others, not certain as to whether the dinner gowns worn will be elaborate or simple, prefer being quietly rather than over dressed. When a lady wears a conspicuously grand costume upon the first night of her arrival, the other guests are sure to follow her example on the second night, in which case she would appear at a disadvantage unless she had more equally good apparel with her . . .'

'A country house party . . . lasts only four nights, the guests arriving on the Tuesday in the week and remaining until the Saturday . . . From September until February are the months in which country house parties are held; after February until Easter there is little or no country house visiting, the reason being that the shooting is over and the racing has not recommenced. In the Easter recess a few country house parties are given, and again at Whitsuntide, and throughout the year from May to November . . . Country house parties are never given unless there is a raison d'être for doing so, sport is the never failing attraction to the gentlemen as is a ball to the ladies . . . For a visit of four days a married lady would require three evening gowns, three morning gowns and if she adopted the expensive habit of wearing tea gowns she would require two of these . . .'

'For an ordinary visit of three or four days, a lady who is accompanied by her maid and therefore requires no special service, is by

no means called upon to give the housemaid anything; if she prefers
to do so, half a crown is amply sufficient. If, however, she be alone,
and the housemaid has given her some assistance, the gift may vary
from 5s to 10s. If she rides and has been out more than once, 5s
should be given to the groom and 5s to the footman who has brushed
her habit. If he has not done so, half a crown is ample remuneration
for cleaning her boots and carrying up her boxes. No other fee can be
expected from a lady, and these are ample. I have heard wonderful
stories of housemaids who refused silver and footmen who demanded
gold. All I can say is, that in a somewhat long and very wide ex-
perience I have never chanced to encounter any of these rapacious
persons; and although I do not doubt their existence, I believe they
are only to be found in the houses of *parvenus* and *nouvaux* (sic) *riches*.'

LATEST PARIS FASHIONS.

'The anti-alcoholic people are so persistent that one is almost ashamed to say in certain circles that one will take a glass of wine. A thrill of horror passes round the dinner table at hearing the once familiar words, and a Pharasaic toss of the head indicates plainly the feeling of superiority which animates the breast of those who drink nothing but water.'

'You must not be led away by any of the nonsensical accounts in the newspapers into the belief that the game of polo or hockey on horseback as played at Windsor on Tuesday, was anything like a success. A lot of rushing about and concussions, no one hitting the ball, but everyone else's legs as hard as they could—an undignified scramble showing how inferior the most graceful Englishmen are in horsemanship to Asiatics. It is a whim of the day, but there is no chance of it coming into vogue.'

The outside world impinged very little upon the lives of the readers, but there was in every issue one or more leaders which covered an aspect of politics, either at home or abroad. It was very rare for the paper to take strong sides, except on absolutely clear cut issues. The usual manœuvre was to discuss some subject of topical interest, and relate it directly to the women themselves. The Government were seldom criticised and politicians were never attacked. There was no cult of personality. On the whole, it might be said that authority was placidly accepted.

Ambulance class at the Alexandra Technical School, Sandringham

The two subjects upon which *The Queen* felt most strongly were the women's vote, and women's education. On the other hand, it is noticeable that never at any time did the newspaper become even faintly militant in its feminism. It was a magazine of fashion and etiquette, a social magazine, therefore one that subscribed, by its very nature, to the superiority of men. They did not wish to rule the country, they merely wished to establish their rights, and in particular their right to a more interesting life, rather than anything more dramatic. General opinions reflected in the leaders, therefore, were more inclined to be the natural ones of the day, rather than anything strictly feministic.

They made a perfectly sensible presentation of the case for the vote, but sometimes they went too far in the opposite direction. When the Debating Society of the Young Ladies of Girton voted by 27 votes to 14 to abolish the House of Lords, *The Queen* became indignant: 'By the great majority of sensible people debating societies are viewed with unconcealed contempt. We can imagine nothing more calculated to make advanced female education ridiculous than that the Girton girls who but recently left the nursery should have debated the desirability of the abolition of one of the three estates of the realm.'

They were prepared to admit that, while they believed in women's suffrage, they realised that the great body of women did not want it.

Printing office established for the employment of women

THE LATE EARL OF BEACONSFIELD.

Benjamin Disraeli

It was apparently thought that because there were about one million more women in the country than men, the whole business of government would be handed over to women, should they get the vote, and there was no doubt whatever that the great majority of women did not want to dabble in the duty pool of politics.

Socialism was naturally regarded with great abhorrence. When faced with something of this sort, *The Queen* was inclined to retreat into rather inexact argument. 'Socialists say that Christianity in this country is merely the chloroforming agency of the confiscating classes.' But they simply did not take Socialism seriously. When William Morris died, they were interested in him primarily as a poet,

secondly as a decorator and last of all as a Socialist. 'A great man has gone out to use the significant Anglo-Indian expression. William Morris is dead. Unless it is Swinburne, he has had no equal since Tennyson died, as a maker of poems in rhyme and meter. He was one of our greatest artists in verse. He was quite a respectable artist in colours. He was something of an architect I believe, and he exercised more influence than any man on what is called decoration. He was not in touch with Bohemia proper, though many from his Socialist camp were Bohemians also. William Morris illuminated their grim sombre lives.'

Home affairs predominated over foreign affairs. The leaders on these subjects were notably dull, though sometimes revealing: 'Lord Salisbury paints a very painful picture of London with their thousands of families having each their single room, where they eat, sleep, multiply and die . . . Miss Hill denies the existence of any class of people whose habits are not improvable or that should be scattered abroad. In noble words she says: "If you move the people, they carry the seeds of evil with them."' On occasions the leader writer would get fiery enough to attack more seriously. '*The Times* declares that the inferiority of the City Police to the Metropolitan body is notorious. We affirm that the exact contrary is the fact and we appeal to the columns of *The Times* to prove our case. About three months ago, *The Times* was in a state of alarm about the inefficiency of the police to prevent garotting. Where did the cases of garotting appear? Every one of them in the Metropolitan district . . . Take again the scandal which has for years past made London conspicuous over the worst governed of continental cities for the brazen effrontery with which Vice exhibits her hideous mien nightly in the streets of the West End. Who is there who knows anything of London life that does not know that this shameful and degrading scandal is entirely due to the corrupt connivance of the Metropolitan Police?'

It is articles on foreign affairs which reveal more than anything the attitudes of Victorian women. They were witnesses to the creation of the British Empire, and as such they had a very definite view of the superiority of Britain over all other nations, in precisely the same way that they had a certainty of the superiority of the upper classes over all other classes. First of all, they liked kings. It is noticeable that in the American Civil War, there being no king to support, they emotionally favoured the South, though common sense told them that the North would win (important factor), and that the North was more likely to be right. The thought, however, of colonial houses in

'Honourable Members' (*1862*)

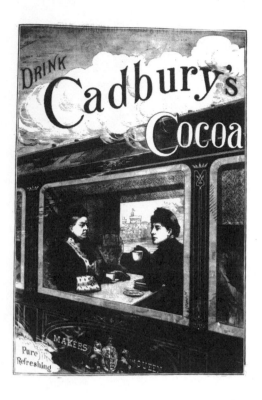

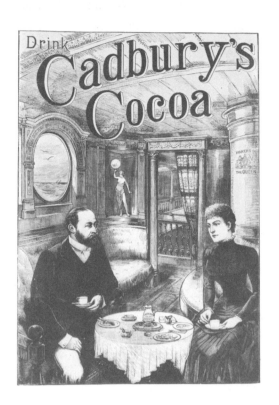

the deep South and of an aristocratic society was too much for them and, if they did not openly express their views, it was very evident beneath the surface that they longed for the South to win. The Franco-Prussian War was regarded merely as tedious inasmuch as it interfered with visits to the German Spas.

But a king or an emperor was the thing – this they understood. Even the death of the Queen of Madagascar was worthy of note, the more so because it enabled them to comment once more on the excellence of the Bible for people in foreign parts: 'Ranavalona II's death will be regretted by all friends of humanity and progress. The reign of the first Ranavalona was marked by three sanguinary and prolonged persecutions of the Christian natives. Amongst the reforms which will render her memorable are the abolition of trial by ordeal, the abolition of slavery as far as the Mozambiques are concerned, the observance of Sunday, and polygamy discountenanced by Royal Decree. Heathen symbols have been abolished and the Bible placed in a position of honour.' They agitated themselves considerably on behalf of the Emperor Maximilian, and the absurdity of his ever having gone to Mexico was glossed over in the horror at regicide. At the end of the century, the old-fashioned concept of monarchy comes slightly into conflict with the gentle sprouting of new ideas. The final comment on the coronation of Alexander II of Russia in 1883 is indicative of a change of mood: 'It is to be hoped that his reign may be marked by internal social improvements, rather than by victorious conquests of his less powerful neighbours.'

The building of the Empire created new problems. Suddenly the Victorians were faced with a world in which they were the rulers, and consequently a world in which their unpopularity grew each year. In 1897, *The Queen* was sadly aware of this: 'A good many people have been exercising their wits lately in the Press on the question why we are not more loved by foreigners. I wonder at the expression "why we are not more loved", when we are not loved at all; when we are hated by almost all nations, loathed by some, ignored by others and only tolerated by the world in general because we are vastly too strong to be kicked out of it . . . I regret to say that Anglo-Saxons are perhaps the least sensitive people existing . . . The Editress of Travel thinks that the chief native cause of irritation towards and dislike of English ladies while travelling lies in the question of ventilation . . .' 'Strange though it may seem it is nevertheless true that we English are *not* considered a generous nation abroad.'

From Notes on Nursing (1862)

Ethiopia
France
England
North America

The Irish question troubled *The Queen* only at the most superficial level. They were shocked, but they were also put out at the effect it had on social life: 'The columns of our daily papers devoted to Ireland give every day a list of murderers and brutalities inflicted not only on men but also on unoffending animals that would disgrace the records of the most barbarous actions . . . Social arrangements are interfered with, the hunting is interdicted. These occurrences are but samples of the anarchy and tyranny that prevails.'

The colour problem was beginning to be noticed. The British attitude was plain. 'The problems of the government of countries in which the inhabitants are of various races is one of exceedingly difficult solution. Whatever may be the beliefs amongst Christians on the one hand and Socialists on the other, as to the equality of all members of the human family . . . the English are about the last people who as a body have acted upon such a belief. The whole question is most serious in America. The white race, the highest in intellectual development and in the arts of life and civilisation is in danger of coming into actual contest with one of the races of lowest development. Fusion between the two races is impossible, and that the higher intellectual race will submit to the lower because they are more numerous is hardly to be thought of. The situation is one which can only be viewed with great interest and anxiety by all well-wishers for the future of the human race.' They viewed the suppression of other races with equanimity. Darwin's theory of the survival of the fittest came in most agreeably, and certainly the leaders of *The Queen* were not troubled by any noble savage complex: 'The world, which was formerly comparatively, is now almost completely under the dominion of the white races, and civilisation is extending to the uttermost ends of the earth. The struggle for life and existence has not altogether been without its evils. Many weaker nations have gone under, and the fight between civilisation and barbarism is another example of the survival of the fittest. The Tasmanians for example, have been removed by the civilised Christian races from off the face of the earth, not one single example of the thousands that peopled that large island being now in existence. There is little doubt that before the forthcoming century shall have passed away, the whole of the aboriginal inhabitants of Australia will have been constrained to follow their Tasmanian brethren.'

They were satisfied that they were right, that it was Britain's duty to rule the world, and to see that her kind of justice was done wherever they happened to govern. Here is *The Queen*'s account of

the start of the Boer War: 'The Boers, being impatient of British rule, migrated across the Vaal, and formed the South African Republic whose boundaries were strictly defined by the Convention of London in 1889. It has unfortunately happened that the Government (of the Transvaal) instead of being what is generally understood by a representative republican organisation, is a tyrannical oligarchy, ruling not only over the natives, but also the civilised foreigners, who are termed Vitlanders, in the most offensive and arrogant manner. The discovery of gold in the district around Johannesburg has led to an immense increase of population in that district. The Vitlanders far exceed in number the Boer population, but the legal, political and social disabilities under which they have been placed become utterly intolerable. The refusal of the government of the Transvaal to ameliorate their conditions has led to the commencement of the present war. The behaviour of the Boers to every race of mankind, whether civilised or uncivilised, has always been one of the most arbitrary and offensive character. Even at the present time the Boers are as tyrannical and as insolent as possible to all persons not of their own race. The letter from a Boer which appeared in *The Times* is an amusing illustration of this. He states that the British race is rapidly decaying; that the children are born weak, diseased and deformed; and that the major part of our population consists of females, cripples, epileptics, consumptives, cancerous people, and lunatics of all kinds, who are carefully nourished and preserved. This clarification will hardly ensure the sympathy of all women for the Boer cause. War is always an evil, and however much its recurrence must be regretted . . . South Africa . . . has rendered such a proceedings imperative.'

Before the War was finished Queen Victoria was dead.

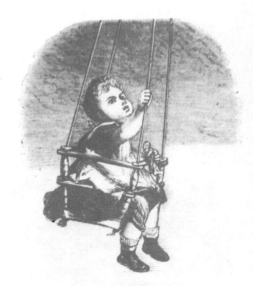

The Royal Vault at St. George's Chapel, Windsor

The Edwardians

The QUEEN

The Ladies' Newspaper AND COURT CHRONICLE

*There is only
one society sin nowadays –
that is to be poor.*

There can seldom have been a universal change so sudden, so marked,
so definite, brought about by the death of one person, as the trans-
formation wrought upon England by Queen Victoria's dying. She
was the age; with her it ended, and the new century was looked upon
with lonely suspicion. Queen Victoria was indispensable to the way
of life which had been created round her, and no-one could envisage
what the new life might be.

There were very few people alive who could remember England
without her. In spite of her age, they believed that some miracle
would save her, but die she did. The country went into mourning.
It was claimed that all international jealousies and voices of discord
were silenced in one united sentiment of homage. In America, the
Stock Exchange and public offices were closed and all principal
thoroughfares hung with black crepe. In France, state visits were
cancelled and the fleet at Cherbourg flew their flags at half-mast.

For a month the magazine was almost entirely devoted to anec-
dotes of her reign, tributes to her as a monarch and descriptions of
her funeral. Each section of the paper tried to credit Victoria with
having given her sympathy and support to its particular sphere. It
was difficult to say that she showed great enthusiasm for outdoor
sports, but it was asserted that she did have a very *marked* preference
for angling. Cycling was in a class of its own: 'Her late Majesty's
tact, foresight and broadmindedness were never more conspicuously
shown than when she ordered a tricycle in 1881.'

'*The late Queen
and her Great Grandson
Prince Edward of York*'

A change was inevitable in England's way of life. When it came it was a violent one; not so violent at the time as it seems to us now, nevertheless it was only a matter of a couple of years before an entirely different note crept into *The Queen*. The whole concept of womanhood changed, and the most noticeable effect was the large number of new subjects which were admissible for discussion. The Edwardian woman was the first to compete in the *demi-monde*, or at any rate to forsake the role of châtelaine and enter society on her own, instead of being a domestic adjunct to a family party. She was not always successful but, weighed against her counterpart of twenty years before, she made considerable headway. At first the attitude of the paper was one of mild admonition: 'A bachelor who invites ladies to tea at his flat or to luncheon on his yacht is careful to invite a relation also, or some married lady of a certain age, and does not consider two young married women without their husbands to be sufficient chaperones for each other from a critical point of view. An invitation to tea at a man's flat or at an hotel when given to only one lady is not a compliment to her. She is either too old to be attractive or too unconventional to need consideration on his part.'

The idea of an open affair with a man was still unthinkable. 'Women should strenuously and fiercely cling to the conventions and not overstep them for the sake of any man that ever lived. To take only the commonsense view—nothing higher—the strongest woman will find herself utterly alone, while the partner of her indiscretion still has the entrée to his friends and a place in society forever denied to her. In an excess of magnificent, but misplaced, generosity, she may count the world well lost, but he never will. She can never be sure of him, for his friends, instead of deserting him as hers will have deserted her, will do their level best to make him treat the affair lightly and to assure him of their support and a welcome when he chooses to break off the unwise connection.' Within a few years there was considerable licence. 'One of the social questions of the day and one that is freely discussed in society, is with regard to the propriety and wisdom of married ladies dining alone with married men and bachelors at fashionable hotels and restaurants, and also of their being their companions at the theatre and after at supper at well-known supper restaurants, Prince's and elsewhere. The sober minded —not the prudish or the strait-laced by any means—are asking is this as it should be, and what has brought about this remarkable change in society life which is so prominent in all sets, and not confined to any particular division. Many causes have contributed to the

The Edwardian era brought married women a new freedom

present position taken up by married men and married women. The facilities now offered for dining in luxury are an inducement—and a very strong one—for men to ask their friends' wives to come and dine with them and an equal inducement to the said ladies to accept the proffered hospitality. Then, too, a still more potent cause has been the absence of thousands of married men from England in South Africa during the last three years, side by side with the voluntary absence from home of young married men to indulge in sport, shooting and fishing, and extended travel in all quarters of the globe.

*The tango tea hour
at Prince's*

Whatever the occasion of this absence from the roof tree, the wives
are left to themselves, and their kind-hearted men friends—usually
the friends of their husbands—think that the kindest thing to do is
to ask them to dine and go to the play, not with any idea of getting
up a flirtation, but with the intention of giving them a little amuse-
ment in the enforced absence of their husbands. As to the opinions
held by wives on this question, they are as unanimous as are those
of men, and each speaks as she feels and thinks. Some are prepared
to accord the same freedom to their husbands as they claim for
themselves. Those may be considered the advanced division, and
these husbands and wives are perfectly agreed as to their right to do
as they please. It is only the lookers-on, the observant public, who
are not quite as satisfied as they are and who entertain doubts as to
whether this lead is the one to follow, and whither it leads.'

By 1909, perhaps as the result of the example set by King Edward
VII's affair with Mrs Keppel, the attitude seemed almost to be that
anything was allowable for a married woman, providing no serious
scandal or divorce proceedings resulted. Certainly *The Queen* did not
hesitate to print photographs of King Edward with Mrs Keppel.
The glamorous young married woman was the centre of all social
functions. Many dinner parties were held in fashionable restaurants,
for the advent of the young married woman as the leader of society
made the whole tone far less rigid. Dresses were cut lower, young
girls were not so severely chaperoned. They might smoke. 'Why
should not women smoke if they like? If tobacco affords so much
solace to men, why should their sisters, who are more highly strung
and of more nervous temperament be deprived of its soothing effects?
Of course, tobacco can be harmful when it is indulged in to excess.
There is a disease called tobacco blindness, in which it is difficult to
distinguish colours, more especially red. Then there is such a thing
as smoker's tongue. Tobacco also causes palpitation of the heart,
dyspepsia, loss of appetite, blunts the memory, produces a nasty
cough, and the smoker's tongue above referred to may produce
cancer.'

'Girls chaperone each other, or mothers devolve the duty on one
of their number will who answer the call'—mixed bathing was
catching on fast; there was more tolerance about divorce, though
not to the point of wanting to make it easy. There were protests
against the rigours of the traditional Puritan Sunday; gambling was
fashionable, and even young girls took bridge lessons from
professionals.

*Mr Max Linder and
Mlle May in the tango*

'Felinda is emancipated, she is quite of the new century. This means she goes out in the evenings without an escort, that she smokes occasionally, that she is interested in sociologies most picturesque phases—but it does not mean that she is not as charming, with it all, as if she were wholly innocent of the ways of the world.' Thus *The Queen* summed up the typical young woman of the Twentieth Century. Certainly it did not mean that she was as charming, with it all, as she had been twenty years before.

The old Queen had lived too long, and, as she had stunted the development of her son by her longevity, she so stunted the natural growth of her country. The conventions she had imposed had been all very well for the world of fifty years before, but they did not fit in with the dawn of the scientific age. The young prince had been powerless before his accession, and after it he was too old to provide the new climate of thought which should have come with the inventions of the late Nineteenth Century. For want of a new creed, the Edwardians exaggerated and caricatured the less rigid beliefs of the late Victorians.

The readers of *The Queen* were uncertain where they stood. They were still the same people: '*The Queen* is par excellence the newspaper of country houses, so I take the opportunity of laying before the wives of peers and squires a royal road to temperance among the villagers on their estates.' The paper wavered between a really conservative admiration for the aristocracy, and a furtive liking for the vulgarity which they condemned.

'Who remembers that *noblesse oblige* and *la démocratie permet*? It is the fashion today to talk of social duty and the right to live but nobody has the courage to say that we belong to different worlds and cannot therefore view things through the same spectacles. These days we can never do anything simply. Now, even the porter and lift-boy have weekends.'

The defence of the aristocracy became almost feverish: 'The idle rich has become a byword of the moment, but to those who know, this term seems a rank injustice. In real truth, people in a high position are often the most hard-worked class in the community. This bitter abuse of the upper classes is cruel and unjust, and bids fair to become a danger to the nation. Centuries of power and wealth have given us the chance to perfect our social system. The English aristocrat has a just sense of his responsibilities, and has always been willing to give service in return for privilege. Let the Socialists rail as they will, our upper classes are the finest body of thinkers and livers in the world.'

The Chatsworth House Party, January 5th 1900.
Back row, right: Queen Alexandra
Front row, left: Hon. Mrs Keppel

At the same time, it was possible for the paper to write in a slightly envious, if frivolous way about the smart attitudes of society: 'If you are very rich you may be gibbeted (in velvet and a luxurious suspended chair) as often as you like and no one will think the worse of you. Yet another sin is to take your own husband about with you instead of some other woman's; and to wear a smile on your face and to seem to think life worth living is also hopelessly vulgar.'

Brittleness was the keynote of the first decade of the century. The premisses by which the fashionable world lived were the same as they had been for fifty years. The chief concern of the paper was naturally with clothes. 'The open-air life is a far more wholesome sign of the times than the innumerable changes of costume that so many up-to-date women make the chief object of their existence. Look what happens at a country house visit. A breakfast gown to begin the day with, some gorgeous sort of *déshabillé*, half dressing-gown, half tea-gown; next a walking dress, short skirted, tailor made; then a luncheon dress, reaching its greatest heights at those ladies' luncheons limited entirely to their own sex. The last will serve also for the bridge party, the wide, really reprehensible popularity of which has produced a new version of Pope's bitter satire, and which runs now that every woman is a gambler at heart, instead of (or as well as?) a rake. There is an especial bridge coat or light jacket for players who sit down to the card table at some impromptu game organised at a morning call. The tea gown was especially invented for that comparatively modern meal, and after it we come to the unlimited varieties and vagaries on which fashion runs riot nowadays for the adornment of the fair sex at dinner, theatre and ball.' But even in the fashion pages, new problems arose with the changing standards: 'The remarks current in society respecting the very low dresses worn by some ladies at theatres and at dinners in hotels and restaurants are not of an admiring nature but distinctly otherwise. While shoulders and necks, beautiful though they may be, seem a discord when displayed at crowded restaurants, where the tables are so close together that the waiters cannot help breathing over these fair visitors as they hand the different course to them, and men distinctly disapprove of this being possible.'

Breakfast was nothing without devilled kidneys, broiled chicken, savoury omelette, kippers and eggs and bacon to choose from. Lunch meant two entrées, chicken and two puddings. Dinner could be anything from five to twelve courses. Wine was essential. The Edwardians drank far more than the Victorians. The paper was

King Edward VII at Balmoral

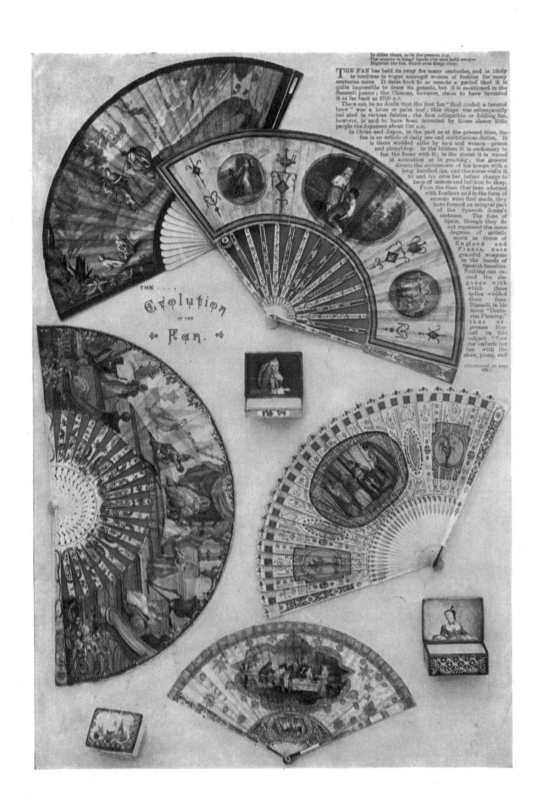

The Evolution of the Fan.

constantly supporting temperance laws, slyly adding that of course these were meant for the poor. They themselves were above drunkenness but not above a lot to drink.

Their lives, as may be judged from this, were, if not as rigorously controlled, at least as parochially circumscribed as those of the Victorians. Their new liberties, far from softening class distinction, if anything hardened it. Already one gets the feeling of riches without responsibility or, at any rate, if there were responsibility then responsibility ignored. The rise of the Socialist party and of the Trades Unions meant that the lower classes began to assume the proportions of a threat. They did not, in the eyes of the rich, acquire a personality as yet, but whereas *The Queen* had before talked about the poor as a nebulous body, they now began to be more aware of individual problems. There is more talk of social work, of slums. They detect that the situation may vary from borough to borough in London; they notice that there is an unemployment problem; they begin to be afraid of the reforms which are being made. Free education for instance is suspect and was virtually condemned as useless: 'The lower classes are, as a whole, unambitious and incurious; they seldom realise the advantage of improving themselves by further education and they do not learn either to use their hands, to read steadily and with purpose, or to think.' What sense is there in educating them if they are not going to do anything with the education given to them?

The Edwardians came to be much tougher than the Victorians, who looked upon charity as a moral or at least a social duty. They blamed the poor even more severely than the Victorians had done, believing that poverty was the result of idleness and improvidence, and therefore the only effective method of dealing with it was coercion. In 1905 about one person in six belonged to the slum class. There were at that time 14,470 paupers on the books of the London unions every Saturday, and the cost of pauperism for the year 1902–3 was three and a half million pounds. 'Of course, this is far too high a proportion, but the noise they make and the trouble they cause is largely in excess of their numbers. However, it is chiefly for them that the rest of the community has to provide policemen, workhouses and prisons, and all the paraphernalia of repressive, remedial and philanthropic organisations . . . Dramatic measures will be necessary before the greater part of the evil can be stamped out.

'In the first place, let it be accepted as an unbreakable rule never to give money to beggars nor food or clothes to tramps . . . Another

principle which will have to be enforced more and more is that of making parents responsible for the upbringing of their children. Public opinion, unfortunately, is not yet ripe for the principle of preventing certain persons, such as lunatics and criminals, from propagating their species (though, we doubt not, it will come in time), but Society undoubtedly has the right to say to a parent you brought these children into the world and you must feed them.' It did not occur to them that the society in which they lived was in any

'Dainty Lingerie'

'Suggestions for the Bathing Season'

way to blame for the plight of the poor. There was no evident solution, unless it were a Socialist one, which was unthinkable. Sterilisation of unfit parents was more and more frequently suggested. 'We cannot admit for a moment the right of men and women to beget children when they have no reasonable hope of supporting them.' Certainly there did seem to be a great many children born who were unwanted. When Parliament granted the Foundling Hospital £10,000 and made it a condition that every child must be accepted, a basket was hung at the gate. On the first day, 117 infants were placed in it.

The Edwardians also blamed Socialism and, in particular, the Trades Unions for poverty, claiming that the Unions drove trade away by their greed: 'One can have no sympathy with those of the working classes who by their own actions, their greed, laziness, class selfishness and unpatriotic behaviour have killed or driven away the trades that supported them . . . we feel bound to condemn the meretricious and fallacious talk of the right to live or the right to work.'

The more serious conditions became, the more ruthless the upper classes became. They believed, consciously or unconsciously, in three theories which justified their attitudes. First, the creed of the Victorian liberal which, watered down, was popularised by Samuel Smiles—that each individual was responsible for his own salvation, spiritual and economic; secondly that failure and poverty were caused by the flaws and weaknesses of the individual's character, and were therefore signs of moral turpitude; and lastly it was positively unfair for the State to use the taxes paid by the successful and good to help those too lazy to help themselves. 'Why should the hard working, thrifty classes work the harder in order to support and continue a class and system of which they disapprove?'

Added to this was a diluted and perverted Darwinism. The catch phrase, the survival of the fittest, was taken to mean that it was somehow necessary, inevitable and right for civilisation's failures to be left by the side of the road while the strongest marched on. Connected with this, was the fashionable belief, mentioned above, in eugenics as an explanation and solution. The bad (i.e., the poor and the criminal) it was thought, would produce bad children, not because of the environment in which they lived, but because their criminal characteristics were hereditary.

The contempt in which they held the lower classes was strangely violent: 'The upper classes merely lose their tempers after a Puritan

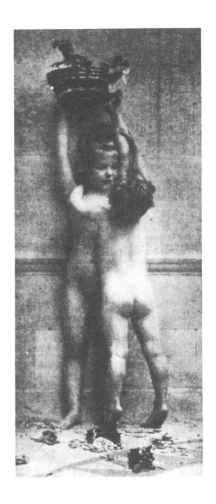

Sunday, and the ones amongst them who think for themselves become unsettled in their allegiance to Christianity. But the lower classes frankly get drunk.'

By the end of the first decade of the twentieth century the Trades Unions had shown their strength, the Labour Party had invaded Parliament. It became clear that voluntary contributions of the rich to charity were going to be superseded by taxation. What had been given as a favour was going to be exacted as a right. That was regarded by *The Queen* as ridiculous. In 1910 a leader protests that 'the returns of voluntary subscriptions and legacies to Hospitals, missions etc., for the past few years, just issued, are a blow to the Apostles of Socialism who are continually demanding that much of the duty of citizenship and many of its privileges shall be divorced from the individual, and undertaken by the State, for they prove that the voluntary system of support for British charities is financially sound and perfectly adequate for legitimate demands . . . That such a society (the Social Welfare Association) is deemed necessary and desirable is in itself yet another example of the ceaseless, unremitting and self-denying interest taken in the care of the poor and suffering by England's wealthy, leisured and cultured classes.'

In the same way that the poor were condemned more harshly, so also *The Queen* became violent against criminals, lunatics and all underdogs. The voice of *The Queen* developed a shrill note in all its denunciations. The self justifications grew muzzier in attacking almost rabidly all social reform — old age pensions were an inducement

to idleness and dissipation; workmen's compensation would lead to faked accidents. Care of lunatics, certainly not worth the taxpayers money, was cash sunk yearly spent on poor, useless and even dangerous derelicts of humanity.

This ruthlessness of the Edwardians was a reflection of more than just the threat from the lower classes. It stemmed also from the Imperialist obsession. The Empire was now built, and the upper classes believed that they had built it with their own hands. They were convinced that it was the greatest Empire ever created, and never ceased to tell everyone so. The Victorian era had, as it were, practised Empire; for the Edwardians, Imperialism was a creed. They believed that they were right to have and to hold British territories and markets by force, if necessary, and that Britain really conferred an inestimable boon upon the subject races. They genuinely thought that England had a God-given civilising mission: 'If the enormous territories held by us are to be occupied, held and developed, we must resume the export of brave men, ready to fill the waste places of the earth, and where government falls on the shoulders of our race, we must take up the burden with a stout heart and full confidence in our national future.' They were hurt when the ungrateful subject nations did not recognise the benefits they enjoyed: 'The present agitation against the British in Egypt is peculiarly unjustifiable and ungracious to us, and injurious to the great mass of the population. For we are in Egypt by no fault and no wish of our own . . . Egypt has never before been so well governed as under Britain.

'The Order of the Bath'

For her sake it is our duty to remain there, and the best friends of Egypt are those who counsel her to come more not less under the beneficial influence of Great Britain.' They claimed that 'the knowledge that the Sahib, the Pale-Face Brother, and behind them the Great White Queen would keep their word both for good or ill, for reward or punishment, has done more for the effectual subjugation of the wildest tribes than all the guns or warships and the bayonets of British soldiers'. They did not wholly neglect the guns and bayonets. 'The Army is called upon every day to defend our rights or extend our influence in various quarters of the world.' They considered the native as inferior in mental capabilities to themselves. 'The native has a very small modicum of developed brain; he is, as Cecil Rhodes once truly said, half child, half devil, and wholly animal, with the instincts of all three, namely a keen sense of justice and an innate respect for his superiors . . . In our treatment of the native we should by all means be kind, but above all, firm.'

Kipling was the poet and populariser of Imperialism and he had endless imitators. In the last words of a serial called *The Imperialist* the hero says: 'I see England down the future the heart of the Empire, the conscience of the world, and the Mecca of the race.' The blacks were infinitely worse than the yellow: 'So often we hear that South Africa is not a woman's country, but few of us who make the statement or who listen to it stop to analyse the reason. The chief reason is obvious, and is one which is a crying disgrace to us. It is the so-called black peril. I do not want to exaggerate, but I do want to look the evil fairly in the face and not shirk facts. In any part of South Africa if the man has to be away on business, a woman dare not and should not be left alone . . . Much has been said and written about this evil but too much cannot be said, and for the sake of the women of England, for the sake of the country's future, and for that of the men who want to make it their home, this matter should be dealt with instantly and severely. Death should be made the penalty for any outrage on a woman, or a hard flogging in cases where there may have been extenuating circumstances. The pampering of the native, these light sentences of imprisonment which for him have no meaning, will if continued, ruin the country for the white man.'

In its enthusiasm for the Japanese at the end of the Russo-Japanese war, *The Queen* offered this as its view: 'With a forbearance worthy of all honour — and imitation — Japan has behaved in the most truly Christian manner to her Christian foe, and for once and all exposed the hollowness of the Yellow Peril bogey . . . Japan will now be able

The Royal Box at Ascot.
The King talking
to the Duke of Connaught on the left,
the Queen on the right

Lord Kitchener

to pursue the even tenor of her way unharassed by bullying neighbours and unfettered by combinations of greedy rivals.'

But for all the self-aggrandisement, there was always a certain
unease. Even as early as 1903, when the War Commission reported
on the Boer War, the leader writer was constrained to wonder
whether everything was quite as it appeared: 'The state of things
revealed by the three volumes of evidence taken by the Royal
Commission on the conduct of the late Boer War is not only humilia-
ting to all interested in the officers and heads of the British Army, but
distinctly disturbing to one's faith in the invulnerability of the British
Empire. Fortunately, to use the words of a so called statesman, we
muddled through the recent war, and somehow came out successful
in the end; but at what an appalling sacrifice of life only those who
lost relatives in South Africa can realise . . . Nothing, fortunately can
be alleged against the personal conduct and never failing gallantry
of the British officers in the field. All the sham of mismanagement
and consequent disaster is attached to the headquarters at home,
and especially to the Minister for War.'

England was becoming, against her will, more closely involved in
European politics. As this happened it became clear that Germany
and not France was the enemy. There was a growing fear of Germany's higher production rate, even of her high birth rate, and this,
incidentally, was one of the factors which restrained too strong
advocacy of the sterilisation of the poor.

If England was to maintain her position, her workmen must work
at least as hard as those of her rivals. Any suggestion that the
Edwardians were unaware of the possibility of war would be absurd,
but for them it remained always an intangible possiblity — a possibility
that was never going to come off. By 1910, the arms race had begun
in earnest, and *The Queen* was even interested enough to publish a
series entitled *Our Dock Yards*. It also advocated compulsory military
training. Occasionally the paper would go so far as to consider the
prospect of sudden attack. An artist's impression in 1911 of London
being bombarded by Zeppelins was captioned, 'From various parts
of the country we continually hear reports of mysterious aircraft
having been seen at night passing over our towns. Are we likely to
have such a disaster as the picture depicts, and what would be the
result?' The actual possibility of war, as opposed to the imagined
possibility, was diminished in the minds of the Edwardians by their
complete confidence in their own superiority to every other race.
There would never be any doubt as to the outcome of any war. The

General Sir Redvers Buller, V.C.
The King of Portugal

truth was that they had reached a point of technical advance to which their imaginations had not yet come. The horror of total war had yet to be experienced. It could not be foreseen.

In home politics, *The Queen* started to take a greater interest. The women's vote was still the natural, primary concern of a woman's newspaper, but as an elegant woman's newspaper any undignified or exaggerated behaviour was to be deplored. 'As believers in the right of qualified women to exercise the franchise for the election of Members of Parliament, we deeply regret the scandalous scenes enacted last week at the Palace of Westminster. For the rowdy, riotous behaviour of the suffragists in the precincts of Parliament affected not only their particular claims but discredited the cause of women's rights in general. To stand on the streets and shout, to lie on the floor and scream, to refuse to leave after abusing the hospitality of the place and yet forcibly object to removal therefrom is not only

Miss Eleanor Ormerod, the first woman to be a member of the Royal Meteorological Society

unreasonable but a disgrace to the sex and breeding of the demon-
strators.' Side by side with this went the other obvious concern with
politics—that of keeping the Socialists down. Up till this time, it had
been extremely rare for the paper ever to take sides in discussing the
affairs of the nation. Liberals and Tories were, after all, upper class.
A few people might take the matter very seriously, and one marquis
might refuse to meet another on account of his views on home rule.
But this was good blue-blooded stuff, and *The Queen*, although Tory
by inclination, did not comment on such squabbles or take part in
them. But come the Socialists, and here was a very different affair.
Even the Liberals came to be thought of as almost too close to the
Socialists for safety. During the 1910 election, the paper said: 'At
the time of writing, the General Election is not yet over, so judgement
must be suspended. As was predicted, the North of England—with a
few bright exceptions, has gone solid for Free Trade and the present

*Suffragettes demonstrating
at the Houses of Parliament (1900)*

*'London's Latest Method of Locomotion.
The New Electric Tramway
from Shepherd's Bush to Southall' (1901)*

'Modes for Motoring'

*The Duke of Connaught
in his Motor*

Government. But it cheers one to know that the dockyard towns are
Tory, and that the Cathedral cities and many of the counties have
returned to their old allegiance. Never has London been so keen on
politics. Mothers in Mayfair and Kensington sent out their children
with sandwich boards on which were the words Vote for Lyttelton
and Vote for Hamilton. Then our evenings have been spent reading
Election results on the sheets at restaurants and Music Halls. And it
was of keen interest to note the cheers that greeted a Unionist win,
as against the chill silence with which news was received of a Liberal
victory . . . London has returned some Liberals but the Tory spirit
still holds sway in the heart of our Empire.'

The Queen managed in this instance, as it would manage more and
more as time went by, to ignore the facts in an effort to console itself.
The cheers which greeted a Unionist win in London restaurants were
not going to be enough to drown the clamour of the working classes,
indeed were already not enough. The paper allowed itself to support
absurdities, which twenty years before, it would have ignored. Later
in that year, Ellen Countess of Dysart was commended for speaking
'a few words of wisdom. She pointed out that Socialism was the
veriest tyranny which would fall heaviest on the working classes. The
rich would migrate.'

With the new brittle, less down-to-earth attitude of the Edwardians
came also a sophistication which the Victorians had never had. The
scientific age in which they lived became more natural to them. They
were no longer in awe of discoveries, no longer frightened by inventions. Progress was to them something which had only just begun,
whereas their fathers had hailed each development as if it were the
ultimate perfection. The Edwardians saw clearly that they were only

A balloon race
at Ranelagh (1907)

*£10,000 Air Race
at Brooklands (1900)*

on the threshold of the modern age. 'Everything we have done in the nineteenth century is as yet imperfect. We have widened the streets, paved them and lit them (as yet very imperfectly) . . . the telegraph is going to do without wires; we are going to talk to each other half way round the world; we can kill at seven miles. Hooray! Here indeed opens up a glorious vista. The nineteenth century has been remarkable for the beginning of things. The twentieth will have its hands full carrying on the works of its predecessor.'

The motor car was established. It is interesting to compare two leaders on speed, the first 1903 and the second 1905: 'The extraordinary intensity of feeling amounting to animosity aroused against scorching motorists and even against automobilism itself, was shown by the treatment of the Motor Car Bill on its passage through the House of Commons last week . . . The main provisions of the Motor Car Bill enact that the maximum speed on an open road is not to exceed 20 m.p.h. Drivers are in future to be licensed and the car registered, though there is to be no test of efficiency on the part of the driver . . . We think that no reasonable person can do other than approve of these restrictions as to speed and the provisions for regulating motor-car traffic. If people want to fly through space at a greater rate than twenty miles an hour, they may travel by railway train; in any case, they have no right to imperil the lives and limbs of their fellow users of the highway by furiously driving at such a

speed that they cannot negotiate or avoid the ordinary obstacles to be met with on roads which everyone has the right to use.'

'How safe and inoffensive cars are when driven carefully and at a reasonable pace was amply proved by the recent trial of the Automobile Club. The average pace worked out at about seventeen miles an hour, which must have meant that 25–30 m.p.h. was frequently reached in the open. Yet there was no suggestion of danger or inconvenience to anyone.'

The air, too, would soon be mastered by man: 'Ever since the mythical days of Icarus and Daedalus men have tried to imitate the action of a bird in flying through the air, and the fairly successful trial trip by Mr Stanley Spencer's new airship would appear to show that the problem, if not yet completely solved, is within measurable distance of solution.' In 1909 a *Queen* correspondent made a flight with Wilbur Wright: 'Up we went as high as a large hotel until the spectators were wee specks below us. I sat in that marvellous construction, my skirts tied round my ankles by a thin cord, and nothing between me and eternity but a few planks and a rest to my back. We seemed to cleave the air like a great bird at a speed of some 40 m.p.h., until we returned to the ground with great precision. "As soon as I knew you were English," Mr Wright remarked, "I knew you wouldn't fuss," which I took as a great compliment.'

In some senses, the Edwardian outlook was broader, in the same way that morals were less strict. King Edward's journeys made it almost a necessity to go abroad in the summer. The paper also recommended winter holidays—ski-ing at Davos or St Moritz. The Swiss and German health spas with their casinos were at the peak of their popularity. The new emancipation of women was evident

The King on his Holidays at Homburg

The Promenade des Anglais, Nice

at the five o'clock *thé dansants* in the lounges and restaurants of continental hotels. Cruises also were becoming fashionable, but were criticised in the paper as being noisy and uncomfortable. A particularly noticeable change as a result of this broadening of ideas was the new attitude towards the Americans. The Victorians had thought them uncouth, graceless and *nouveau riche*, with no table manners, no breeding and no charm. The Edwardians, however, did not patronise the Americans—they thought American women more attractive, wittier and better dressed than English ones. American girls were not precipitated straight from the nursery into social life, and so were better able to deal with the fashionable, epigrammatic conversation on which the Edwardians prided themselves. The only time which the paper does criticise the Americans arises from jealousy. More and

The start for the desert
of an Englishwoman's caravan

more of the aristocracy were marrying them, partly for the advantages already described, and partly because they were rich.

The breadth of interest did not, however, extend to the arts, at least, so far as society was concerned. Intense vulgarity is inimical to sensitivity. With this vulgarity went an admiration for physical strength, at the expense of intelligence. It was possible to live comfortably at home with two servants, eating five meals a day, including a twelve-course dinner on £400 a year, so that the rich were very rich and one of the chief outlets for their money was extravagant sport. Yachts, race horses, cars, grouse moors, were symbols of wealth. Lord Lonsdale used eleven motor cars to transport his Saturday to Monday guests. Often enough, it was sufficient merely to acquire these symbols to be admitted into society. Sir Thomas Lipton was a perfect example of this new attitude.

The question of physical strength was not only applicable to men. The public schools certainly aimed at turning out boys not so much with intelligence as with integrity, but of an inarticulate kind. These qualities could be acquired in the rugger field. Girls too, must be educated to be fit mothers of an imperial race. 'In our girls of well-to-do parentage, we have, probably, the best human material that the world in its long centuries of striving has ever produced . . . Well grown, fresh complexioned, clear eyed, wholesome in body and mind.' It was a greater social advantage for a girl to play a good game of tennis or golf than to play the piano, sing or dabble in water colours. In a serial about Anglo-Indian life, one girl weeps to think that were she at home in England she would be enjoying a game of hockey, instead of enduring the unbearable heat of India. This was the climate for Philistinism rather than aesthetics.

It is interesting, however, that this was a time of great creative activity, and in particular, of great interpretive quality. The upper classes were inclined to ignore it. Shaw, for example, meant little to them. He had a great following but not in society, which preferred the less demanding plays of Barrie and Pinero. The opera was marvellous, with Caruso, Melba, Tetrazzini and Chaliapin. It was also well attended but for social reasons rather than artistic. *The Queen* even noticed that its readers did not go to the theatre for intellectual stimulation: 'The British playgoer is the object of many eloquent ratings from playwriters and players. He is continually asked by these admonishers why he does not attend representations of outspoken pieces . . . He is told he is hypocritical because he will read in the privacy of his own study what he would not listen to in the theatre;

Lord and Lady Leith of Fyvie at Cowes

The new royal yacht, Victoria and Albert

The Royal Military coach at Ascot

that he is puritanical because he declines to be publicly acquainted with some of the vices—and most crushing of all—that he is no artist, because when some plays are given which would fill a continental house he lets the stalls and boxes remain empty . . . The point is that the men and women in the places where full dress is expected of them are unforgettably in each other's presence. There they are, all these people who make their own world, knowing much that they are by way of not knowing, having many a painful secret, many a terror hanging over them which they trust is unsuspected by their neighbours, many a sorrow or disappointment (not necessarily discreditable) which they would gladly forget. And while they are there, seated among their acquaintances, they are no more prepared for the uncovering of tragic truths than were Claudius and Gertrude for the upsetting piece which Hamlet thought fit to stage at Elsinore.'

The ballet was at its height, with Pavlova, Nijinsky, and Karsavina. Painting was similarly ignored inasmuch as it was perhaps the most progressive period which had been seen for many years. The Impressionists and post-Impressionists were still scorned in England, and Picasso, had he been heard of, would have been beyond contempt. What was admired was the dead, traditional style of the English school, with flickerings at the fringes of Aubrey Beardsley. Writing about the New British Art Club an article said: 'The observer to whom the "newness" of the pictures would be anathema would look in favour upon the willows, the cattle, the limpid stream and the sunshine that are the ingredients of early Spring by Mr Mark Fisher, while W. Sickert's *La Vecchia* is gruesome and repulsive, and Mr Lucien Pisarro's impressionist attempts are totally unconvincing. The fault of the New British Art Club is that these and paintings of a similar type should be flung in the public's face under the excuse of being new and modern. The ordinary person with enough knowledge of art to suspect, and suspect rightly, that he is being humbugged becomes irritable and suspicious.' Portraits were still very much *de rigueur*, and the rich commissioned with singular abandon quantities of indifferent artists. It was, perhaps, more good luck than anything else that made Sargent their favourite.

This society, which was based on an able-bodied imperialism, found its acme of expression in Kipling, but even he could be warned not to go too far. 'Mr Kipling's poetry is full of the creative, pregnant quality which is the essence of the Greek word *poiesis*—our poesy . . . To no poet of our generation has such prophetic grace been given as to Mr Kipling. It is he who has made Englishmen turn again from

The Duchess of Devonshire and her eldest son at Bolton Abbey

a kind of national agnosticism to faith in their country. Before Mr Kipling arose, Englishmen were afraid to speak up for England lest they should be taunted with jingoism. It was a disgrace to desire fair play for their country or to be proud of her successes. We were Pharisees, choking with cant. A microbe like the dreaded trichnia was preying on our national fibre. Mr Kipling was the Tyrtaeus who lifted us out of that Slough of Despond, and he is our Tyrtaeus still. But he would speak with hundredfold effect if he would go back to the bugle calls which are heard over the din, and understood of the rank and file, and make thousands move as one man . . . One specially misses the high straightforward bugle note, which transforms men into heroes, in that fine poem "Ubique" . . . Here was a subject which he should have treated as Gordon wrote of Balaclava. But, as this poem stands, though it gives the uttermost farthing of their need to the exploits of the R.A. it is couched in such involved

Women and Sport

language that, bar a gentleman-ranker or so, there is probably not a single private or non-commissioned officer in the regiment who could understand it. Mr Kipling must give up this obscurism if the nation is to derive the full benefit of its most inspired voice.'

The Queen could take a line about the circulation of pernicious literature, and this leader on the subject perhaps more than any other shows the change which overcame England after the death of Victoria. Their new liberty enabled them for the first time to speak frankly of sexual relationships. 'The National Council of Public Morals is doing a very valuable service to the nation by the issue of its manifesto dealing with the important subjects of the declining birthrate, the moral education of the young and the circulation of pernicious literature. Let us consider the question of corrupting literature and the moral education of our youth of both sexes. In dealing with the former matter, it is obviously very hard to pronounce judgement on the delicate matter as to where art ends and immorality begins in any book dealing with the eternal question of the relations

Swimming Competition at the Bath Club

Henley Regatta

of the sexes and how far these may be discussed in popular literature without detriment to public morality.

'It has been suggested that books, and especially novels dealing with sexual problems, the obligations and duties of parenthood, etc., should bear a descriptive sub-title or words to the effect that they are intended for the perusal of married folk only, or for those interested in eugenics or as not suitable for young people generally. But this announcement would attract instead of repel the class it sought to warn off . . .

'The great truth must not only be taught but enforced that the racial instinct exists, not primarily for the satisfaction of individual married couples, but for the wholesome and proper perpetuation of the human family generally and especially that of the British race. It is falsely modest, selfish and cowardly to ignore, belittle or deny the

Lord Howe playing the organ at Gopsall, Atherstone

Enrico Caruso

Jan Kubelik

Thomas Beecham

Miss Lily Elsie

fact of the remarkable position among the races and nations of the world of our British race. It is not so much that we are morally better than other people but that we are better fitted for ruling less developed races than any other nation . . .

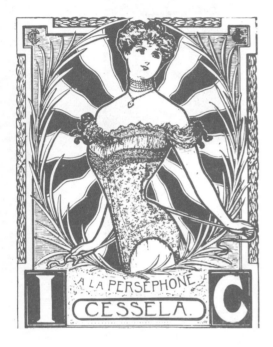

'*When he could retreat
no further, he threw out his hand
with a forbidding gesture*'
(*from a serial*)

'From this viewpoint therefore it is vitally important that our youth should be brought up with a knowledge of what will surely be demanded of them in years that are to come.' Even the act of love in marriage was to be performed for the glory of England.

Night, from the picture by E. Brunkal

The Royal Family of Norway

The Great War

The QUEEN
THE LADYS NEWSPAPER
& COURT CHRONICLE

No. 3682.—Vol. CXLII.　　　SATURDAY, JULY 21, 1917.　　　Office: BREAM'S BUILDINGS, E.C. 4.　　　Registered.—Price 1s

LADY EDEN.

Mentally and morally we all feel
that we cannot give our time and thoughts
to frivolous things.

The Great War was to be the watershed after which the system of privilege would never again have the same power and meaning. An acceptance of inequality had been built up over the centuries. Four years were to be sufficient for its undoing. Privilege might survive in one form or another; but no one would much longer believe in the right of the aristocracy to its possession.

In 1914, however, the spirit was as it had always been. They could not foresee the cataclysmic effect which the war would have upon society any more than they realised what a twentieth-century war would mean. The English still lived in a dream of chivalry, in which it was possible to write:

> 'And when we sees all our sailor folk
> And our soljer lads with their bands go by,
> Us waves our 'and (tho' us feels a choke),
> And us gives a cheer (tho' us wants to cry),
> Oi says 'tis 'mazin what stuff comes out
> Of the best us be, when a war's about.'

It was to be a long time before attitudes caught up with the technical advances which science had made.

The same confidence, which enabled them not to question the security of their domestic affairs, blinded them to the state of world politics. As early as 1910 *The Queen* was saying that Germany had everything to gain by a war and we had everything to lose, and to expect her to curtail her *Weltpolitik* would be naïve. Yet the actual

*The Tsar with General Williams,
head of the British Mission to Russia*

*The King at the front,
with General Pétain*

outbreak of war was a source of amazement. In August of 1914, the paper said: 'The tempest of war has arisen in four days from a cloud no bigger than a man's hand.' Considering that *The Queen* represented a class which prided itself on its knowledge of foreign affairs, this amazement is surprising. The murder of the Archduke Franz Joseph at Sarajevo had called forth only an article on the beauty of the requiem service—no political significance was noticed at all. The upper classes had such faith in the power of English direction of diplomacy that they believed that no major war could be embarked upon without their specific sanction and approval.

The general belief was that the war, though unexpected, was certain to be over in a matter of three months. 'Military experts seem agreed that the war will have three successive stages; the Naval struggle in the North Sea which may have begun now and should be definitely decided within ten days. In about a fortnight's time will come the crisis of the campaign in Belgium and the French frontier—this should be decided probably a month from now. Lastly, in about six weeks time the colossal Russian armies will meet the German and Austrian troops in Poland. We shall have much to endure before three months are over.' They could see no reason to modify fashions, to restrict entertainment—indeed, no need to stop doing anything which they had enjoyed before the war. 'It is so interesting, as the war brings us more and more vivid pictures, in letters from the front, to see what modern fighting is like.' This was the essence of it. The war seemed to be a vast military tattoo staged for their entertainment by the gay, golden boys, as Mrs Katherine Tynan described them, who would finish the matter before it became tedious, or the restrictions irksome. The whole thing was a lark in which everyone played soldiers—saluting officers, watching parades and sneering at the 'disloyal shirkers' who had not joined the glorious fight. The image was full of stirring pictures of national confidence.

By the early months of 1915 a depressing change overcame London. What was to have been a brief frolic of a war showed no signs of ending. The original excesses of patriotism all wore off, leaving nothing but the dreary routine. 'Christmas leave has come just at the psychological moment when a danger zone has been reached, when the first novelty of army life has worn off, the first enthusiasm has spent itself and the bands of rigid discipline have been drawn tight enough to pall.' The magazine's purpose then was to try and shake its readers out of their gloom. Enemy advances were glossed over, and a major victory was claimed every time the allies

regained any ground, but already there was no denying the fierce lists of casualties which poured in daily. 'Last year we had a seemingly endless store of unused energy to call on, and it was used lavishly. This year we know that our national energy like the nation's supply of gold must be used with economy and care.' Rumours were rife, pessimism gripped the land, 'Men received castigation the other day for allowing themselves to be affected by the depression at their clubs. They were bidden to lend no ear to the gloomy gossip or to melancholy statements of prognostications made by fellow members.'

A regular appeal to save food

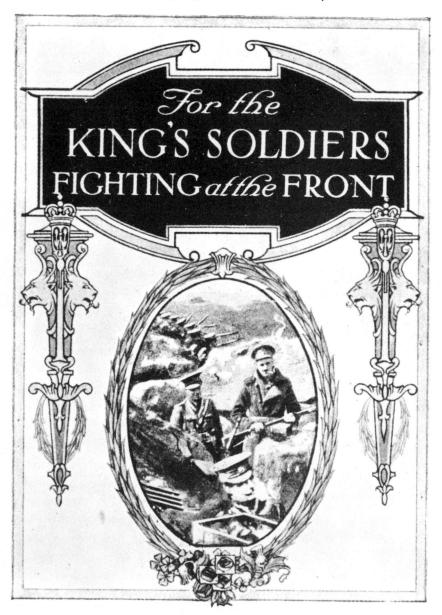

Receiving the Royal
Christmas cards at the front

To make it worse, the depression was very largely voiced by intellectuals and thinkers. Influential men talked pacifism, and it was a far cry from the nineteenth-century wars fought between rulers, wielding professional arms. For the first time in history, the civilian population was called upon not only to die but also to make sacrifices at home. Austerity campaigns, rationing, state interference in production — these were the horrors of modern war, which cast down the patriotic optimism of the first months of 1915. The result was that misery came to be highly prized, and women seemed almost to take a morbid pleasure in thinking that they must enjoy nothing. Anything that might alleviate the gloom was frowned upon as frivolous; all energies must be preserved for one's country. 'Mentally and morally, we all feel that we cannot give our time and thought to frivolous things . . . to remain sane, brave, pitiful, yet calmly determined to do our part in the nation's work is the duty of us all.' By now, even fashion was affected: 'The new fashions are certainly appropriate to wartime. If the truth may be so much as hinted at, men would probably be found to be thinking that their women folk are rather dowdy.' Even an urge to play tennis was dismissed as flippant and unworthy: 'Few people would actually like playing tennis now, since there is always a sense of unreality which accompanies all attempts to go on with work at these times.' None the less, this spirit could not last — the war was bringing with it a new age, one in which the suffragette movement would be proved to have been right. Women were needed. Now at last they had a chance.

They seemed after a while almost to be enjoying themselves. They engaged in war work with tremendous enthusiasm. By the middle of 1915, many more had applied for employment than could possibly be used. Their zeal tended to exceed their capabilities, so there were complaints of a shortage of women trained to do or capable of doing really useful jobs. For a start, therefore, they had to be satisfied with knitting body-belts and mufflers, and other comforts for the trenches, packing up cigarettes and soap, and starting schemes for teaching French to the wounded. There were also some 70,000 Belgian refugees to be looked after, and it was considered rather a delightful adventure taking them into their houses. 'Even lone women, who were allowed to refuse to take soldiers or officers, have only in a few cases exercised their privilege.' Gradually, their work became more serious, quite apart from the V.A.D. and nursing, women were employed as chauffeurs, railway porters, factory inspectors and even in the making of aeroplanes. They also had to do their housework, which was not

Evening toilettes

*Children of the Corps Diplomatique
at a charity party in the Hotel Cecil*

regarded as being so romantic. Housework lacked glamour, and
while they were always able to claim that the upper classes showed
their true grit and superiority in the way they stuck to their jobs,
they found themselves depressingly incompetent about the house.
Militant feminism was no longer necessary, and when in 1918 they
were given the vote, this was looked upon as a natural outcome of
their wartime activities and created very little stir.

While the status of women was changed, so was that of the poor.
The same men, who twenty years before had been regarded as unre-
generate rogues, were now absolutely vital in the war effort. They
were the ones to become the gay, golden boys, bound to their officers
by the common bond of Englishness. 'Us and the poor are in this
together.' Everyone was in it. Everyone was to economise; everyone
must queue; money no longer bought everything. The upper classes
faced these facts with gallant fortitude—meals were slashed to three
courses; there was no meat at breakfast; margarine and custard
powder found their way even onto upper-class tables. Men servants
were considered a luxury. The simple life had its charms (although
not having servants was tedious when you wanted to be not at home),
and in doing your own gardening you suddenly discovered how very
much more your garden produced. In the spirit of common endea-

vour it seemed almost as though class barriers would crumble,
unnoticed. 'When this war is over, the returning soldiers will have
none of the class distinctions of the country for which they have
fought outside her inviolate frontiers. They have given orders to men
outside of them in the social hierarchy; they have taken orders from
those once beneath them; the whole standards of life have been
transfigured, and the whole life to which they return they will
transfigure too.'

The bogey of the savage poor was dispelled, and the advertisements spoke proudly of the soldiers' love of soap and cleanliness. In
an excess of enthusiasm, they envisaged a Utopia which would be
created after the war. The cult of the Royal Family, as we know it
now, began during the war. Suddenly the monarchy by sharing
austerity, and by working at war charities became a step closer to the

*The Endell Street Hospital
was staffed entirely by women
from the Chief Medical Officer
to the porter at the gate*

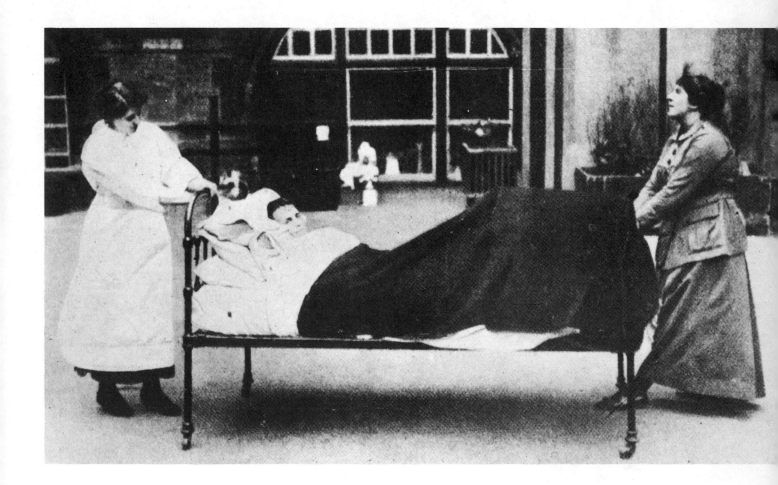

*Lady Katherine Thynne
with wounded soldiers in the
hall at Longleat*

*Lady Monson with eggs
for the wounded*

public. The inflationary spiral gave the illusion that the working
classes were richer. In fact, the cost of living for working-class families
was, by 1918, about 80 per cent above normal. The housing shortage
was to be dealt with. 'Relief of overcrowding is a measure of safety
not to be neglected and not to be left under the present difficult circumstances to unassisted private enterprise.' It was even possible for
a regular woman feature writer to argue the socialist case in *The
Queen*: 'One of our chief national duties is to carry into the peace era
some of the improved methods of work which war compelled us to
adopt. The establishment by the Government of certain big industries
was one of the good things that war gave us . . . Unless public production is continued, we shall suffer great troubles from unemployment
on one hand, and from loss of national opportunities on the other.'
The Editor made it plain in the next issue that these remarks were
the responsibility only of the author, but it is remarkable that they
were ever printed.

It was not only in the political field that life was changing. Three-
quarters of a million jobs by 1916, formerly done by men, were now
filled by women. This produced a great change in their actual way of
life. It was no longer unusual for women to live alone in flats, and the
term bachelor girl was coined to describe this army of newly-inde-
pendent women.

The war created its own particular problems of etiquette, and, in
particular, induced a general relaxation of formality. It became perfectly possible for a hostess to introduce to one another two guests in
her house. Before, this had not been possible at all, for no hostess

Women on the land

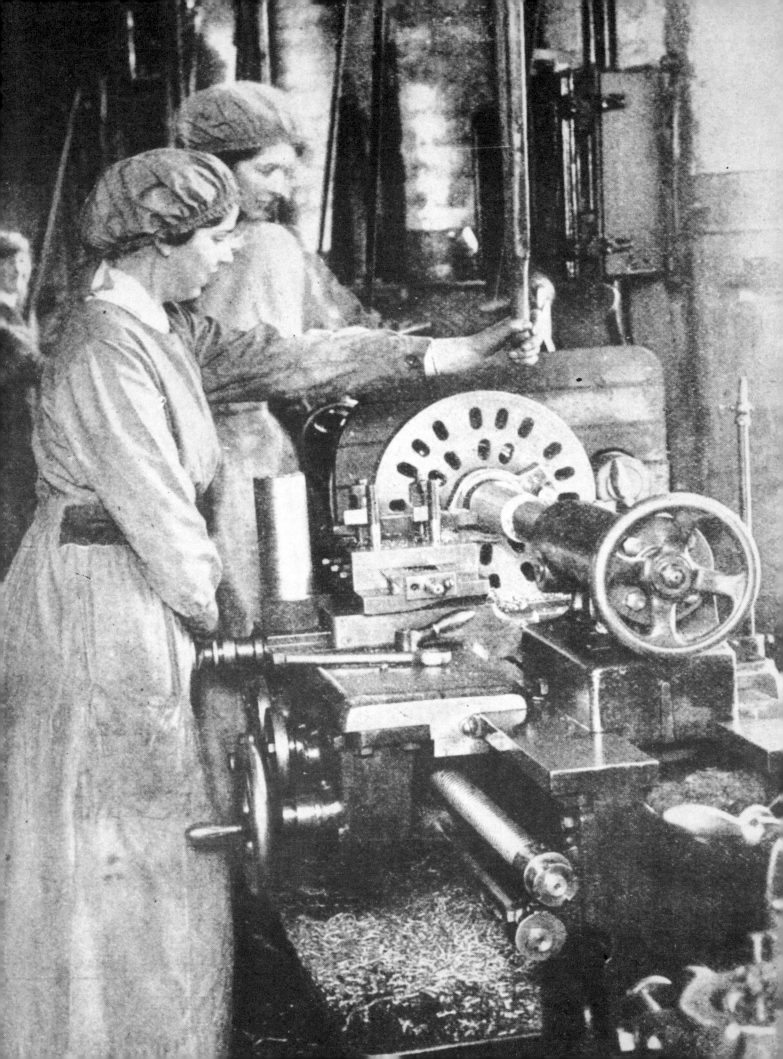

would have cared to assume the responsibility of starting an acquain-
tanceship between two people who might not wish to know one
another. Even clothes were affected by women's new status as
workers. Their skirts in the day-time became shorter and shorter. In
the evening as well, dressing habits became more lax. 'A feature of the
restaurants, even more marked than the prevalence of khaki, is the
frequent appearance at dinner of semi-evening frocks, and even those
which can by no stretch of imagination lay claim to their title.'

The very restrictions themselves, which wartime imposed on the
upper classes, seemed to be levellers. The black-out at night and, by
1918, the 9.30 curfew meant that all classes of people went to
matinées. The theatre was popular, Somerset Maugham drawing
huge crowds to the box offices, and Tchekov becoming fashionable.
The pantomime too, with its opportunities for joining in the singing
of 'Tipperary', 'Keep the Home Fires Burning', 'The Long, Long
Trail', and so on, was emotionally popular. But while the barriers of
actuality were being broken down, there began to be built the barri-
cades of fantasy. The fact is that they were all in it together, and
there was little time to assess the structural changes which had come

Women in a munition factory

Mr Lloyd George's driver

Women police

over the country. The upper classes suffered, therefore, from two main delusions. First that the end of the war would bring a return to the same standards which had prevailed before it, and secondly that the English way of life was indisputably the best. An incidental outcome of these beliefs was the almost obsessive loathing of the Germans which was engendered in the newspapers. Anything with the slightest taint of Germany was taboo. Nobody could own a dachshund; German composers were held in some contempt: 'Presumably the Allies cannot boast a composer worthy to please the élite. Everybody knows that Schumann wrote beautiful music, but a trifling compliment might have been paid to creative musicians other than the Teuton.' Spanish was substituted for German as a second language in schools, a photograph of a perfectly innocent-looking German soldier was published with a caption describing him as typically brutal. More important than this was the clinging of the aristocracy to what they regarded as their rights. While it was all very well to muck in, they were determined to resist any serious incursion of their privileged status. It was now, perhaps almost more than in Victorian or Edwardian times, that the seeds were sown which were to lead to the

The Queen and Princess Mary at a matinée for wounded Irish soldiers

Prince Henry after the steeplechase at Eton

The Duchess of Rutland

The Prince of Wales by the Duchess of Rutland

Prince Edward of York.
2 months old.   White Lodge
                       Richmond

V.9

bitter class warfare of the twenties and thirties. They had no intention of abandoning any of their prerogatives.

While the afternoon bridge at homes gave way to working parties and knitting parties, while Claridges was used for emergency war concerts, it was in 1915 still possible to go abroad for a holiday. 'Biarritz, in particular, is quite as easy to get at as ordinary towns.' Later, in order to go to the Riviera or Switzerland, say, it became necessary to get a doctor's certificate and a special visa, and this was by no means difficult. The paper complained that the sad consequences of the Zeppelin raids was that the fireworks on the Fourth of June at Eton must be abandoned. Dances were held quite readily — so much so that the King expressed disapproval of too much merrymaking. The result of this protest from the throne was typically expedient. Married women's dances for those no longer in their *première jeunesse* were stopped, but the equivalent of deb dances continued — a reflection of the practical attitude of the upper classes, for these dances for young people served the important purpose of getting them married off. But throughout all this, there was a note of grumbling. Once the fervent patriotism was past, the kind of fevered relic of Edwardian imperialism which allowed a feature writer to say, 'I have said it before and I say it again and again, those dead who had their chance to die thus are to be envied, *envied*, from the bottom of our hearts, the hearts of us who sit at home in safety while they

Sarah Bernhardt
after reciting a war poem
at the Coliseum, 1916

A portrait of the
Countess Mathieu de Noailles

Royal Academy Private View:
Lord and Lady Desborough

'*Kultur has passed here*'
from one of forty cartoons by
M. Louis Raemaekers

'*A brutal type of German soldier*'

die for us'—once this spirit had gone then a dissatisfaction set in. Perhaps most typical was *The Queen*'s view of petrol rationing. Everyone was limited to sixteen gallons a month; the motoring correspondent wrote: 'No distinction is to be made between large cars and small; so that the allowance of 16 gallons a month may mean 500 miles of running to one owner and only 150 to another. This might be equitable enough if every owner had known what was coming when he bought his car, in the same way that he knew that a big car would involve him in a higher engine tax than a small one. But inasmuch as he is paying the higher tax it is the reverse of fair that the owner who contributes 20–40 guineas a year on his car to the revenue should only be allowed as much petrol as the one who pays three or four guineas.'

There were complaints about the difficulties of entertaining: 'The position of a town hostess in this time of war is not a very enviable one . . . There are many reasons for this. The strict rationing falls heavily upon all classes; so stringent is it that it is almost a matter that weighs on the spirits of all. It affects every meal of the day—breakfast, luncheon, tea, dinner; indeed the present Controller is of the opinion that afternoon tea should disappear from the family circle altogether, and he would have a fragile luncheon, a still more fragile breakfast, and a dinner that does not merit the appellation of such. It is needless to say this opinion is not shared by the general public. . . .

'It may be that the large reception rooms have to be shut for lack of service and of fuel, and that the radiators, which kept the house so warm, can no longer be fed with anthracite coal; this expensive commodity being in use in the kitchen, burnt in a special stove, costing the modest sum of £25—modest, no doubt, in the eyes of the Coal Controller, but not so in the eyes of the hostess.'

The end of the war when it came, was received with a surprising calm. Mr James Beck, an ex-Attorney General of the United States visiting England at the time of the Armistice said: 'You were nobly great in the hour of disaster, and you are supremely great in the hour of victory. I have been here a week and have not yet heard one syllable of vain boasts or vindictive hatred. In New York, when I left, the bells were ringing, the whistles blowing, and pandemonium reigned to celebrate the surrender of Austria and Turkey. But you remain silent in your hour of triumph. England sees her most formidable foe at her feet, and never a shout proceeds from her lips. It is perfectly amazing to a stranger.'

The paper reported 'London kept high holiday on Saturday and Sunday. The Lord Mayor's Show with its marching troops, its Waacs and Wrens and Wrafs, its cheering crowds in the streets and patrolling aircraft in the deep-blue heavens, was a strangely fitting celebration for the day. It was said, on seemingly good authority, that the crowds exceeded in magnitude any since the first Jubilee, and certainly there was no room to spare! Sunday again saw more orderly, quietly jubilant people crowded in dense masses around the ranks of captured guns and all round Westminster; the King and Queen had a rousing reception when they drove amongst their people in the afternoon. By a happy inspiration the King was in naval uniform, for the Senior Service claims him very specially, and it is that Service which has made victory possible, as those who know

Pre-war impression
of a Zeppelin raid (1913)

Don't let a Zeppelin

catch you in Curlers

Have Natural Wavy Hair and look your best under any circumstances.

most, realise most fully. And on Monday when news of the signing of the Armistice came, London gave itself up to rejoicing. Flags sprang from nowhere, work and traffic was reduced, if not suspended, and crowds of cheering people streamed along, waving miniature Union Jacks and singing the *Rule Britannia* which means so much to us—and to the world—today.' *The Queen* did allow itself, if not a shout, a healthy crowing, entitled *Babylon the Great is Fallen.*

The peace stretched ahead with awkward uncertainty. Prognostication about the future was rare, partly because of the wish to think that nothing had changed and partly from no understanding of what might come.

Complete resumption or total destruction of their way of life seemed to be the only alternatives for the upper classes. They fingered their way through the first year of peace, at first optimistically, then with an offended detachment.

Peace was a disillusionment. It was neither triumphant nor dramatic. Peace was for the first time no longer the opposite of war. At home, change was gradual but relentless and disheartening. Abroad, treaties, reparations, pacts, re-shaping, a new kind of ending to a war. Victory was not much to shout about.

'A silhouette at Sulva:
early morning tea.
Official photograph circulated on behalf
of the Press Bureau'

The Twenties

The QUEEN
THE LADY'S NEWSPAPER
& COURT CHRONICLE

No. 3824. Vol. CXLVII   SATURDAY, APRIL 10, 1920   Registered. Price 1s

A NEW PORTRAIT OF H.M. QUEEN MARY.

Our social conditions
are in the melting pot with
so much else today.

The war over, a new way of life had to be found. The response to the completely upturned situation which faced England in 1920 was almost trite in its obviousness and simplicity. There were three main attitudes which governed the thinking of *The Queen* at this period. First, an aggrieved resentment at the changes in the way of life of the upper classes which they saw not as a necessary development, but rather as a rebellion almost to be compared with the French Revolution. The only relic of the wartime comradeship with the working classes was a rather hideous relationship between officers and their soldier-servants whom they kept on in private service. Secondly, an even stronger need than the Edwardians had felt to escape into frivolity. Lastly, an extravagant admiration of youth—the result of so many of the young men of England having been sacrificed in a war, the winning of which produced none of the security which had been expected from victory.

The old way of life had gone, and it had not been gone sufficiently long for any comfortable compromise to have been reached. The old standards by which society might judge its members were now useless. The attitude of the nineteenth century had been tough; the aristocratic class had few challenges—conditions of membership were rigid. In a society where land was the primary yardstick of social standing it was easy to decide who was and who was not eligible. The system of primogeniture had meant that younger sons with no land or prospects sank quickly to anonymity. The great estates were preserved intact by the eldest sons, and it was next to impossible for

outsiders to break in, at any rate, without a long apprenticeship. But now a new situation had arisen. Swift fortunes were being made; estates were crumbling; there were not enough of the rich aristocracy to go round. A different formula was needed by which to establish whether or not a given person was a member of society. The new criterion could only be breeding. By the creation of artificial customs and taboos, society was able to preserve itself without having to admit the *nouveau riche*. It was no longer a sin to be poor, as it had been in the Edwardian times — in fact it was now almost respectable.

The Queen was still read in country houses, but the country houses were losing their glamour, and were becoming burdens for those who lived in them. Keeping them up meant except for the few, restricting activities in other fields. There was a resulting mousiness, strongly reflected in *The Queen*. For the first time a pathetic note began to creep in to the upper classes' picture of themselves. They were sincerely sorry for themselves, and in their self-pity they retreated into a snobbery unlike any snobbery yet seen, for it had about it the aura of gentility. Certainly the plight of these diminished grandees was at times real. They had been brought up to believe that they could live in only one way and, more important, that their children deserved a particular kind of education. In many cases, their incomes were decreasing steadily owing to inflation and taxation. In many families there was no husband or father, or even worse, 'the erstwhile bread-winner was ill or disabled by wounds'.

The Queen began quite early to reflect the gentility of the new poor with a coyness which became typical of the 1920s. The new strata of society were classified into Lady Great House, Lady Newly Rich, Mr and Mrs Badly Off and Mr and Mrs Middle Class. Lady Great House had had to shut down all but the best eight bedrooms (and four staff rooms), and kept only a useful maid, a cook, a between maid, a parlour maid and a housemaid, 'while the Newly Riches— rich as they are—do not keep an establishment on the scale of Lady Great House (before the War). They have a housekeeper, three in the kitchen, three in the pantry, a house boy and three housemaids.' It was, however, Mr and Mrs Badly Off who really suffered, although *he* was the second son of the second son of a peer, and *her* family was well-connected. On £800 a year (free of tax) they were compelled to live in a small house on a housing estate and perhaps had to send their daughter to a grammar school. 'Undoubtedly, to them one of the trials of life is that they can no longer afford to mix with their former associates.'

The signing of peace in the Hall of Mirrors, Versailles 1920. By Sir William Orpen

"The Most Awful Spectacle in History."

MILLIONS OF CHILDREN NAKED AND STARVING IN EUROPE.

Every British Citizen Called Upon to Help—But it Must be To-day—To-morrow May Be Too Late.

WITH HUMAN DESTINY AT STAKE WILL YOU STAND IDLY BY?

Another Helpless Child is Dead—Another—and Another—While You Read—And Hesitate!

WE have won the War. We are justly proud. We are spending on our well-earned amusements and our comfortable meals, **millions of pounds every day!**

And all the time outside our very doors, a multitude of helpless children and stricken Mothers are perishing for want of food and clothes—not One Thousand, Two Thousand, or a Hundred Thousand, but MILLIONS! It is not in China or Thibet. It is in Europe—a mere tourist's trip from where you are reading now. It is not due to natural causes which we might regard as Destiny and for which we might feel inactively sorry. It is part of the price which poor, innocent children are paying for the glorious victory we have won.

A TERRIBLE FACT.

Cruel cold and famine are stalking among these hapless mites, without clothing, without fires, without shelter, and spreading their miserable agony far and wide. It is a terrible fact that in some districts there is **not a child alive under the age of 7 years.**

If we stand by and let such things be without raising a hand or spending a penny to avert the wholesale catastrophe, we are for ever humiliated in the eyes of God and Man.

Your opportunity is now. All the channels of relief are organised—part by America under the guiding hand of Mr Hoover, and part by Britain's "Save the Children" Fund under the Chairmanship of Lord Weardale, which has this year contributed £150,000 to help the little ones in all the Famine Areas, irrespective of Race, Politics, or Religion.

HOW WILL YOU HELP?

There are many ways in which you can help—knowing that what you can collect or subscribe will be distributed under the direction of distinguished organisers who know how to apply every penny without waste or misuse.

Lord Weardale will personally acknowledge every donation to the Fund. He is also very anxious to secure the co-operation of Public Men and leaders of Society—anyone, in fact, who has in the past assisted to raise Funds in the form of Local Subscription Lists, Charity Funds, Dances, Whist Drives, Concerts, &c.

Whatever you can spare—however much or however little—is distributed personally by willing helpers of the relief agencies supported by the Save the Children Fund. Every few pence you can so easily spare means a meal for a poor starving child. Every few shillings means warm clothes for a poor shivering, wasted childish form. Every few pounds means shelter rest, change of air, and kindly care for a homeless infant.

2/- will Provide a Daily Dinner for One Child for One Week.

£1 will Feed and Clothe a Naked Starving Child.

£2 10s. will take an Ailing Child

to Switzerland, where kindly **Foster-Parents are ready to give it Three Months' Good Food and Nurse it Back to Health.**

£100 will Feed 1,000 Children for One Week.

The mothers and friends of these starving children know that this relief is British, and every little one saved to-day is a friend for Britain in the future. But it is not for this political advantage that you are going now to loosen your purse-strings. You are going to help because you know the comfort and joy of having saved precious lives and of having justly earned the gratitude of the helpless.

THE UNANIMOUS SUPPORT OF EVERY CREED AND RELIGION.

The "Save the Children Fund" is the only Relief Organisation which has the whole-hearted support of the leaders of every movement, every creed, and every denomination.

The Archbishop of Canterbury says:

"We cannot exaggerate the importance of the appeal for our immediate help. Let the greatness of the need be realised, and the British people will, I am persuaded, do their utmost to stay the scourge."

General Smuts writes:

"It is the most awful spectacle in History, and no one with any heart or regard for human destiny can contemplate it without the deepest emotion. It is a case for a mission of rescue work such as the world has never seen."

Dr. Arthur Guttery (President, National Free Church Council):

"The first duty of the new peace is to

rescue millions . . . . from the threat of starvation. I am convinced that Central Europe is in danger of a famine which may involve all nations in a common ruin. The cry of the hungry can never be foreign to the followers of the Son of Man."

Mr. Hoover (United States of America Food Minister):

"There are at the present moment more than three and a half millions in Europe

who will die if they are not provided with milk. This will have to be done by private charities."

In Europe alone Cruel Cold and Famine are stalking amongst MILLIONS of hapless mites, who are without Food, without Fires, and without Shelter. Is all this terrible Agony nothing to YOU?

SUBSCRIPTIONS ON ACTIVE SERVICE WITHIN 24 HOURS.

Whatever you can spare cannot be too small to be of value to the cause. Every penny you collect or subscribe will be immediately applied to the desperately urgent need of the starving and homeless. Within twenty-four hours your subscription will be doing active good so perfect is the "Save the Children" Organisation—so eagerly helpful are its willing workers.

The great call to our humanity and pity surely cannot fail to stir every generous feeling in our hearts. Pennies count as well as pounds. But **it must be to-day.**

In some towns in Central Europe there is no milk, no fats, no meats.

Babies who are not fed by their weak, half-starved mothers have no food but frost-bitten potatoes.

In most cases they die. But far greater the tragedy of those that live on in this appalling misery. Every week babies are born to people who have literally not one single rag to put round them.

Just think of it you who live your comfortable lives. The memory of those who died in the war of humanity's sake demands your help in this awful crisis. Let us do all we can before it is too late, so that none can say that we have lived, and that our loved ones died in vain.

Your personal subscription or offer of help should be addressed to Lord Weardale, "Save the Children" Fund (Room 173), 26, Golden Square, Regent Street, London, W.1—but please make it quickly, for every moment you hesitate another innocent life may be forfeit.

SAVE THE CHILDREN FUND

OBJECTS.—TO HELP THE CHILDREN THROUGHOUT THE FAMINE AREAS.

PATRONS:

HIS GRACE THE ARCHBISHOP OF CANTERBURY; HIS EMINENCE CARDINAL BOURNE, ARCHBISHOP OF WESTMINSTER; THE REV. A. T. GUTTERY; THE RT. HON. EARL CURZON, K.G.; THE RT. HON. LORD ROBERT CECIL, M.P.

To LORD WEARDALE,
Chairman of Committee of "Save the Children Fund" (Room 173), 26, Golden Square, Regent St., London, W.1.

SIR, I would like to help the Starving Children in the Famine Areas of Europe and Asia Minor and enclose ....as a donation to the "Save the Children Fund."

NAME..

ADDRESS..

....

Queen 15.5.20

There began to appear little niceties of distinction between what a gentleman might work at and what he might not, that is, as was likely to be the case, if he were not equipped to do a serious job. Whereas sixty years before, a penniless younger son would be expected to go out and earn his living in whatever way he might, there now appeared various professions which were not considered demeaning, professions which were the precursors of the antique shop and advertising. Sometimes they became rather more over-enthusiastic than practical: 'We fear that Mrs Dott may be over sanguine as to the profitableness of some of the rural industries to which she directs the attentions of officers. Rabbit-breeding, bee-keeping, basket-making and the like are all very well, but they seldom bring in the income a married and educated man requires.' In particular, women were enabled in their emancipation to undertake work of some sort — titled women began to open little boutiques, and others were praised for their endeavours in equally refined pursuits: 'Mrs Bembaron, a clever craftswoman, occupied herself before the war with designing and mounting bead bags, for which she felt she had a special flair. Not long after the war had broken out, and later when questions arose of reconstruction and of capturing trade for Britain, she was farsighted enough to recognise that in this hobby of hers lay a wide field of commercial enterprise.'

Living in places where no one had ever before thought of living became chic: 'In former days, Putney, though possessed of many advantages, could scarcely be classed as an aristocratic quarter, yet during part of the war a marquis lived and died there; while, if report says truly, a well known peeress is even now negotiating for quite a modest dwelling in Putney.' 'People live in such odd places nowadays, in bits of other people's houses, in mews and in parts of their own country houses. The papers are full of advertisements about labour and space saving furniture as a result of high taxation and high wages, and the dislike of women for domestic work.'

Servants were as ever one of the most difficult problems. The situation became, by the paper's standards, so impossible that the subject was almost too bitter and obvious a one for discussion. 'Food prices and wages of domestic servants are from half to double as much as they were before the war, and despite the vast numbers out of work it is almost impossible to obtain servants. The Reds say that domestic service is degrading — what manifest rubbish.' It was one of society's sorest grievances that the working classes, however badly off they were, would still rather draw the dole than go into domestic service.

'*The lady who obliges*'

The magazine took a more practical line, and labour saving and space saving became common adjectives in selling accommodation and furniture. Women were no longer ashamed of doing things themselves. An advertisement for a mowing machine showed a woman using it: 'The Dennis Lawnmower in action. A lady can work this machine with ease.' Kitchens became compact and shiny, bathrooms white-tiled and hygienic. 'Mr ——, a young architect's idea is that in these hard times there are numbers of people who want six-roomed flats with bathroom and kitchenette and a constant service of hot water — Mr ——, being the possessor of a babe, sympathises with young parents of upper middle class who find it so difficult to house themselves and cannot afford to keep enough servants to run many-roomed basement houses with nurseries at the top.' There were fewer and fewer articles on how to treat servants, or on their welfare. Comment was limited to listing the actual duties of servants as a guide for those who had never had them before, which replaced the previous assumption that everyone had them.

The poor, as the Victorians and Edwardians had known them, had vanished as a concept, though not as a reality. But *The Queen* became less and less concerned with reality. It was so concerned with its own social upheaval that it had no time either to champion or even attack the grievances of the lower classes. Strikes, unemployment,

malnutrition—as starvation was euphemistically called—were barely discussed in the paper, except when they had a direct effect on the comfort of the privileged classes. A curious dichotomy arose in their minds about working-class power. It never occurred to them that manhood suffrage would equal rule by the masses. In this there was the contrary misapprehension to the earlier belief that votes for women would entail the complete assumption of power by the womanhood of England. Together with this wishful thinking that votes did not mean influence, went the belief that they were living in an age of explosion, in which the lower classes would rise up in force and murder them. During one transport strike they claimed: 'The railway semi-strike has aggravated the already unbearable discomfort of locomotion in London, and will not, we are told, be the last of its kind. We are, indeed we all know it, in the throes of a revolution almost as uncomfortable as if it were the kind with bloodshed and rapine.' They did not concern themselves with the cause of the strike, merely with its effect.

Any solution to the problem of unemployment was likely to be a fanciful one. Redundant workers were encouraged to emigrate, but it was appreciated that the colonies did not want, indeed would not accept, any more industrial labour. *The Queen* hit upon a happily ingenious adaptation: 'Why not then, instead of collecting several hundred artisans, collect a small township and send out a nice assorted Noah's Ark with a whole community on board.'

Revolution or not, they were determined so far as possible to maintain their status as the privileged class. There was such uncertainty as to whether they would be able to maintain that position that one notices in their attitudes marked contradictions. They treated some matters with greater seriousness than they had ever applied to them before, while in other affairs they were almost aggressively flippant. The Victorians had almost disapproved of pleasure, even the Edwardians took theirs seriously, but the new generation of the twenties threw themselves into enjoyment with a frenetic, even a slightly desperate, energy.

Dancing became an epidemic. All the big hotels and restaurants, the May Fair, the Berkeley, the Trocadero were providing dance floors. The Blues, the Charleston and the Heebie-Jeebies—whatever the Prince of Wales happened to be dancing—replaced the old-fashioned formal steps. Night clubs sprang up—the Riviera on the Victoria Embankment, the Embassy—and gave the Bright Young Things a further opportunity for shocking their elders.

'*The better way*'

Drawing by Frank Brangwyn

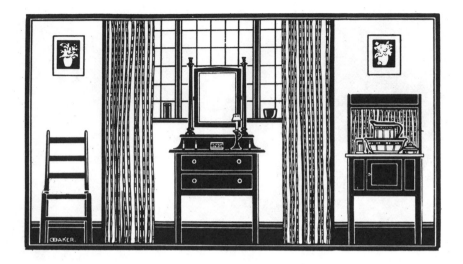

The pre-war scale of grandeur and formality had disappeared. 'A month of the London Season has gone by, but as yet none of the great houses have done any entertaining and compared to the seasons of pre-war days this one seems likely to be unimportant. Royal parties are few and far between, and there seems nothing to take the place of such great places of entertaining in the past as Devonshire House, Grosvenor House, and Montague House.' Nevertheless there was entertaining enough. Young people went to two or three parties each evening; if they were bored at one dance there would be a crippling exodus and they would all invade the party of some other hostess whether or not she had invited them. 'How does one keep a well filled room throughout the evening? Almost everyone may take it into their heads to go elsewhere at the same time. Jack—a modish youth who adorns all the best ballrooms—says the people stay where the supper and champagne are the best, unless there is another dance so socially important that they want to show themselves. Supper should be *à la Russe* consisting of hot soup, fish, chicken or a mixed grill and an ice, and everyone should sup at the same time. You must have enough people, not too many and the right ones. When you have arranged all this, doubtless some of the gilded youth of the day will condescend to favour you with their company.' Hostesses had to choose between an empty ballroom or a room full of guests they did not know. Entertainment was primarily for the young. Chaperones were declining and after her first season a girl, more often than not, went without one. The young were to be encouraged: 'New dancers

*Phyllis Clark
and Victor Sylvester,
dancing instructors at the
Empress Rooms*

*Fred and Adele Astaire
in* Lady be Good.

must grow up to replace the million and a half who sleep forever on the battlefields and a further million and a half who, lame, blind, disfigured and paralysed, still fill a thousand hospitals.'

The star of this social whirl was the flapper. Emancipation went to her head: 'She lives at a pace, which were I not blooming strongly would make my head whirl. An amusing child but oh! so naughty. She does nothing which I was brought up to think a well behaved young girl should do and most of the things she shouldn't. I do not think she has even a bowing acquaintance with a knitting pin, and as she has no personal maid how she manages her clothes is more than I know. But she always looks pretty and charming, if occasionally untidy. I see John looking at her shingled head and her cigarette, and the expanse of banana coloured stocking, which she presents to the world, but he does her bidding with alacrity. Anyone over 35 might just as well be 90 in April's eyes. The elderly dancers who we see make her shriek with laughter. Having received the normal telephone invitation she returns giggling "Love-a-duck! Why *did* I say I would go?" ' If she was silly, the young men were just as bad: 'That evening we went to a dance, very large, very crowded and a young man for a bet ate a whole bowlful of fruit salad. A great waste of a perfectly good pudding. Girls are so silly but I don't believe they are ever quite so silly as young men. There were lots of other good things to eat at the dance, caviar amongst them—although I don't think caviar is right for a dance supper.'

The cult of the young led inevitably to forlorn disapproval by the older generation. The new attitude to sex was criticised: 'Where

'*It was good of you*
to come and see two old women . . .
A fool could see
that you were Bartram's girl,
and that is enough for a Lowrie,'
(*from a serial*)

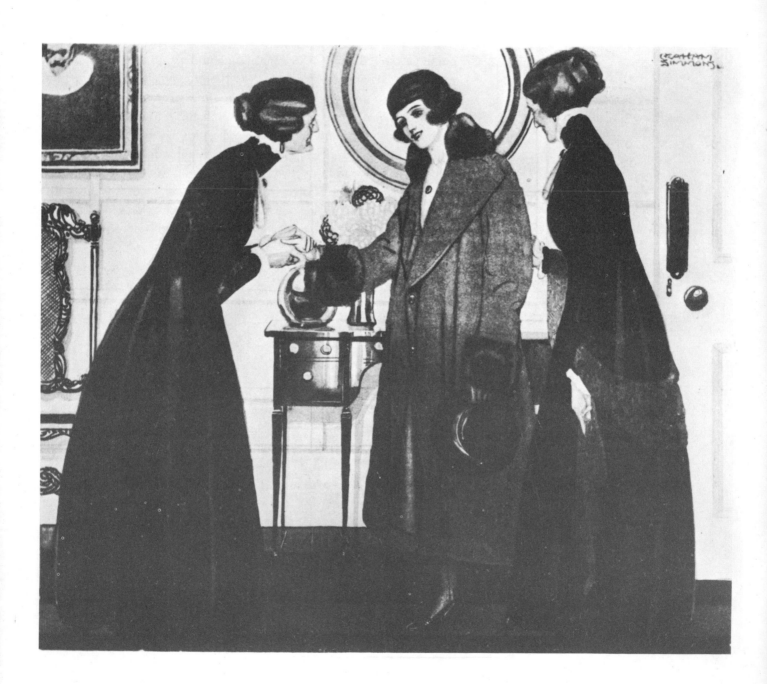

shall we find a Sheridan to incorporate the fashion with modern manners? Alas! Nobody makes a sensation now with a little French milliner. The fashion is for all to be open, all to be in one's own class, and for all to be so bored that though it is high time screens came into fashion, we have yet to relearn that some things should be screened.' The divorce rate was a cause for concern and there was great despair at the rudeness which young people showed towards the old. In one instance it was possible for the parents of two girls to call upon the A.A. and police to prevent the girls going to spend an innocent and unchaperoned day at Oxford with some undergraduate friends. They were turned back by the police at the entrance to the town. But parents could not win in the end. A mother wrote complaining that of course it was the University that spoilt her daughter. 'She is just *longing* to go away and earn money (I won't say her *living*—quite a different thing!) and share diggings and an unfettered life with a chum. She seems to have few intellectual interests, though she reads articles on economic subjects and is always ready to lay down the law, as one having authority, on complicated social problems, which, she implies, we of the older generation could not possibly deal with . . .'

The position of women was entirely changed. It was not only that youth was in revolt but there was also a huge surplus of women owing to the war casualties and many more whose lives must be devoted to widowed mothers and wounded brothers. There were in London

Una, Lady Troubridge, with her prize winners, Fitz John Minnehaha and Fitz John Papoose

'An effective stance: Mrs Le Marchant in play at the Forum Club'

eighteen spinsters to every ten bachelors between thirty and forty years old. The war by killing a generation of men made it impossible for women to be forced back into the shelter of the home. *The Queen* even carried a series of articles on careers: Medicine, the Bar, Secretarial work, Acting, Modelling and Sculpturing.

Representing as it did the staider section of society, the paper was inclined to relapse into resentful fuddiduddiness. It was as contemp-

ORIGINAL
Boudoir
or
Smoking Suit

Original Pyjama in black satin, coat lined with silk, revers of corded silk, vest and collar of white crêpe de Chine, with tucked front, waistcoat of black satin.

PRICE
12½ Gns.

MARSHALL &
SNELGROVE
VERE·STREET·AND·OXFORD·STREET
LONDON·W·1

Mlle Lenglen, the tennis champion

tuous of the other classes as it had always been: 'The other day I lunched at a large restaurant which caters for the middle middle-class, and found that one could obtain food quite as good as that served at smart places at considerably lower cost, but the clients had no more food sense than a pig in its sty.' On the other hand, the temper of thought in the country as a whole did have its effect — there was a slight awakening of social conscience shown for instance by the sympathetic description of the work being done to help unmarried mothers, the writer pointing out that mental attitudes had changed. An unexpectedly strong plea against proposed cuts in education asked: 'How, above all, can we reconcile it with our intention to make this land a land fit, not for heroes, but for anyone to live in, if we go back to the old ignorances and the old stupidities of pre-war days?' At moments they were almost surprised to find that the more typical views which they held were also held by others. They could ask whether there still was a social barrier between the ex-secondary day boy and the ex-public school boy at the Universities. They could even forsee, however disagreeable it might be, a breaking down of such barriers. 'As a matter of fact, in the world outside school these social barriers are rapidly breaking down, as indeed they must in a democracy. Our Labour Government is an example of the fusion of all classes, for every type of school is represented in that body and among the wives of the Ministers.' The paper was confused and so took refuge in an exaggerated admiration of the Royal Family. The first feature every week was entitled Her Majesty's Diary and consisted of a day by day, almost hour by hour, report of Queen Mary's activities. The daily lives of other members of the Royal Family followed in order of precedence.

The general interests of the readers cannot be said to have widened very considerably. The changes in society brought to their notice a few practical aspects of life. In an age of vanishing Nannies, the upbringing of children ceased to be an automatic performance as regulated as a broiler chicken farm. Instead they came to know their children better, and so to discuss education not as an abstract concept but as something about which they had to make actual decisions. Public schools were of course *The Queen*'s answer, both for boys and girls, even if some space was lavished on discussing the alternatives. 'In a really good and well conducted boys' school there is but little room for the development of injurious idiosyncrasies . . . The generally good natured chaff, and even the outspoken reprobation and the pressure of public opinion among the lads themselves, go far

Christening group at Goldsborough Hall.
In front: Lady Harewood, The Queen
with the baby, George Henry Hubert Lascelles.
Back row: The King,
Princess Mary, Viscount Lascelles

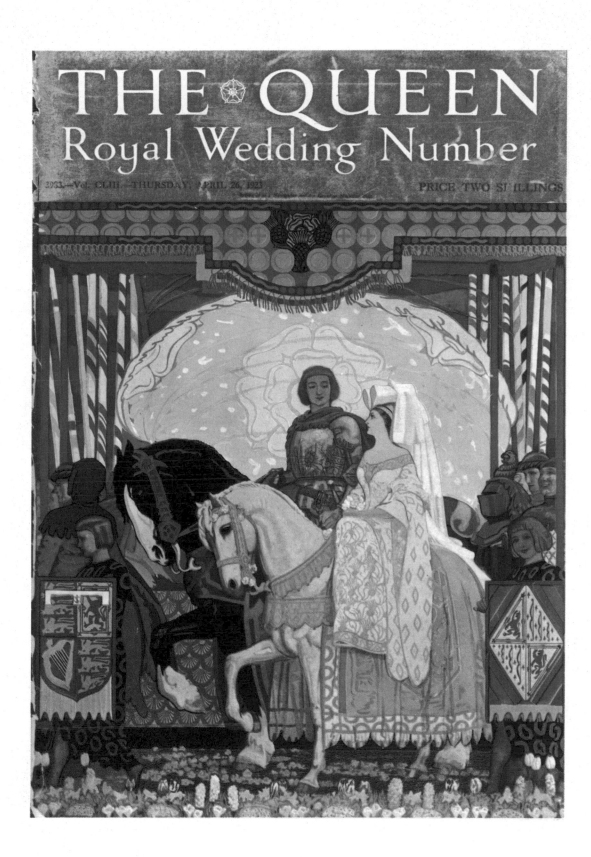

to secure a really healthy and normal state of mental and moral nature. Up to recent years the girls were less fortunate; there was more sentimentality and an undue development of personal ambition, which, together with a tendency for exclusive friendships, did much to mar results. But since girls have enjoyed the discipline of team games, and there has been less tendency to over stimulation of *personal* as apart from *corporate* endeavour, there has been a marked improvement in morale.'

Politics were progressively less discussed over the decade. The vote had been given only to women over 30 and excepting a few feminine agitators there was not much support for reducing the female voting age to 21. The paper disliked the idea, it seemed to them 'to dull the morning glory of twenty-one by dragging it to the polling booth before it wanted to go'. But by 1928 the flapper vote was achieved by Act of Parliament without much fuss.

Women were beginning to be admitted to positions of national importance. Barbara Wootton started her series of committees of enquiry by looking into the national debt. *The Queen* thought it would be a good idea if such women were allowed to use their natural gifts for organisation by running the public services. Directly after the war *The Queen* evinced a natural Conservative vengefulness in its attitude to Germany: 'Our new poor . . . may be tempted to travel out by way of Germany, if they can reconcile themselves to rub shoulders again with ex-enemies. Many of my friends are still horrified by the idea of eating Hun bread, and many who have stayed in German towns tell me that they are made to feel they are not wanted. But courtesy, somewhat fawning, perhaps, is universal.' But they could show good sense: 'The German Empire loses 30,000 sq miles and just one tenth of her population, but while she was utterly humiliated as she deserves to be, she is still left substantially the strongest state in Europe. It seems plain that after twenty years or so of recuperation she will be quite a match for those whom she may then consider to be her enemies . . .' or even a little humour: 'When we ordinary dullards hear any talk of an international loan of £40,000,000 it means nothing much to us. We are now so accustomed to monstrous sums of money that we imagine this sum falling like manna from the bankers, from America, from the Jews, from the air, from anywhere but us. And we have not grasped that the ordinary British Investor is to be asked to lend the greater part of £40,000,000 to Germany in order that Germany may pay what she owes to France, who has no intention of paying what she owes to us.'

The Duke of York
and Lady Elizabeth Lyon

The Labour Party, coming to power in 1924, made the upper classes feel that their already diminishing security was even more severely threatened: 'Few of us realised that we might live to see two great turning points of history during our life times, one international, the result of war, the other domestic and political, the outgrowth of women's suffrage. Now we seem to be on the edge of a third. The old order may be passing away and traditions that seemed rooted in stability may be swept before the Labour broom as mists before the wind.' All the same it did not seem to them that England was totally doomed: 'The end of England? I wonder. If it comes to that, people said the same about the Chartists, yet the reforms which the Chartists demanded have come to pass now without any evil consequences.'

Princess Elizabeth

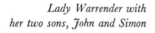

Lady Warrender with
her two sons, John and Simon

Miss Megan Lloyd George

As always they did not like to get too involved in domestic political disputes, 'Wherever one goes the sole subject of conversation is the Labour Government. Personally I have much sympathy with Labour, though none with rag, tag and bob-tail revolutionaries who cannot believe that if they divide the greater part of the wealth of the rich amongst the poor on Wednesday, by Friday there would again be the rich and the poor. Mr Ramsay Macdonald has the courage of his opinions. He held them when they brought him and his family unpopularity and suffering, therefore we hope that he will have strength to deal very wisely with the situation.' Mention of Mr Ramsay Macdonald was one of the earliest comments on a political figure. They certainly would never have criticised one. They even found it possible to champion Winston Churchill. A. P. Herbert wrote a tribute to him when he changed from the Liberal to the Conservative Party: 'Today Mr Churchill's fate is decided. Whatever the individual may think of his views and history, however many bees one may suspect in his capacious bonnet, no fair minded person can help sympathising with this persecuted statesman. No public figure has had so little fair play; no man is more misunderstood by the masses. Because of his political militancy, his undoubtable courage and

Lord Westmorland, Viscount Borodale
and Earl Beatty at Hazelton

The wedding of
Lady Dorothy Cavendish and
Major Harold Macmillan

The Prince of Wales in Cape Town,
with General Hertzog

admitted genius for military affairs, he is popularly imagined as a kind of Prussian militarist, callous and inhuman. He is, in fact, a man of great humanity with a strong record in matters of social reform, though he does not in the current fashion run about the streets proclaiming brotherly love.'

The fear of Communism was very strong, probably at this time as a result of the horror which the upper classes felt at the overthrow of the Russian monarchy and aristocracy, rather than any ideological feeling. This attitude towards the Bolsheviks led them to have considerable sympathy with the Right Wing movements in Europe. The occasion of Mussolini's march on Rome aroused in them only admiration: 'Fascists are patriots. The Communists who spat on the Tricolore signed the death warrant of Communism in Italy. Too many men have died for the Tricolore . . . "A Roma" was the cry . . . Like Crusaders, these black shirted, black helmeted men began their march in the historic land . . . What was astonishing in this delightful and passionate race was the dignity, the order of these men. . . . Benito Mussolini, the leader, like Clemenceau, is a journalist, dependent on his pen and the Lord—*for his daily bread*. He is the son of a blacksmith of Milan.

'The Fascisti promise three things. The defence of the Victory, the Reconstruction of the Army, and Economy, clean to the bone. That is, a life with something of religion, with a patriot's pride, Discipline spelled with a capital D, and Sacrifice, in name, not of class, but of the Nation. It is the first time in the history of New Italy that mass movement has been under perfect harmonious control—direct, *swift and sane*. It is portentous.'

By the end of the decade there was a definite unease about the prospects of World Peace: 'Ten years after the war to end war suspicion and jealousy still stalk among the nations, and those who hoped that great things might come quickly and with little effort after that first Armistice Day are becoming a little despondent. There is no need to despond. Among all peoples there is a steadily growing demand for peace. There is hope, but time is passing. Not always will the international horizon be so clear of a cloud in the shape of a nation definitely bent on aggression. Not always will the men and women be with us who know only too well the obscenity and utter futility of war. The time for pacifism is now when no armed danger threatens.' The general attitude to foreign affairs showed that they had not really learned the lesson of the First World War. They still believed that world politics could be dominated by England.

A portrait of Lawrence of Arabia

Foreigners were still contemptible. 'It is certainly true that French railway employees do lose their heads in time of stress and become hysterical.' One interesting point was the appearance for the first time of anti-Semitism in 1922. It would be tempting to suggest that this was part of the rise of Right Wing feeling, but it is more easily attributable to prejudice and the suspicion of anything foreign—as Jews were supposed to be. In a review of Hilaire Belloc's book *The Jews* came these opinions: 'Mr Belloc's argument is presented with singular temperance and fairness. The Jews are an alien race who have permeated Europe. Their attitude to life is not ours; they do not understand us, nor we them. From this mutual incomprehension friction must result, and is likely to turn itself into violence. The only method of avoiding this is to secure recognition of the difference between European and Jew, and to make the Jews realise that they cannot behave in Gentile countries as they would behave in a country of their own . . . Mr Belloc also calls attention to many points which ought to be better known in England, such as the recent and rapid growth of the Jewish problem in America.' On the other hand a critic adversely reviewing a play made these observations: 'The almost incredible caddishness of the hero leaves one in a state of bewilderment. We are asked, it seems, to laugh at a man who is capable, in his own house, of taunting one of his guests—a Jewess—with her ancestry! (One's natural tendency would be to kick him.)'

Mary Pickford is returning to her old type of part in her new film, entitled " Little Annie Rooney," in which she plays the title rôle, the twelve-year-old daughter of a policeman

Douglas Fairbanks as Don Cesar de Vega, and Mary Astor as Dolores de Muro in the exciting film " Don Q, Son of Zorro," now being shown at the London Hippodrome
(Above, centre) Carol Dempster as Sally in " Sally of the Saw-dust," Griffith's latest production, which is now being shown at the Empire Theatre, Leicester Square

(Right) After a two years' absence from the comedy screen, Charlie Chaplin has at last made a welcome re-appearance in " The Gold Rush," shown for the first time in Great Britain at the Tivoli Theatre, London, this week, and for some weeks to come

Film Favourites in New Productions

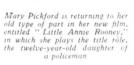

Another scene from " Little Annie Rooney," with Mary Pickford at her most mischievous

A tense moment in " Don · Q, Son of Zorro," the most recent film starring Douglas Fairbanks

H. G. Wells

Scientific progress was treated as a matter of course and not as a topic for discussion in a magazine of this sort. Any references to it were peripheral: 'It seems that the golden silence of the films is definitely to be broken. Miss Mary Pickford is to make a talking film; a number of English actors are training for the talkies; already the Phonofilm Company here has produced a group of sketches—George Robey for example as a barrister, Ernie Lotinga as a recruit—wherein the slickness of the tongue, combined with action suitable to legal and military life, is intended to deceive the ear. I believe the Phonofilm Company does not intend as yet to produce a long, dramatic picture. The public it is suggested is not ready for it. The question is also whether the talkie is ready for the public and whether given the best of all possible conditions it can ever be an improvement on the silent film.'

'Broadcasting is going to save us a lot of trouble, perhaps even that of going to the House of Commons if elected, for in time debates may be carried on through the air. So what if we become slugs? We presume that transmitters providing concerts and so on will send out what "everybody" wants, or what they think "everybody" wants, or what they think it would be good for "everybody" to want, in which case the programmes will consist, not of what is choice and rare, but of what is popular, banal and cheap. Would it pay any business syndicate controlling the wireless lanes of the air to cater for the few, the highly cultured, the discriminating?'

A portrait of his wife by A. J. Munnings

The taste of the twenties is familiar to us. Cubism, orphism, expressionism, surrealism, all these had to be gone through. The ferocious straight line governed all design; in fashion there was the unbroken line, straight, slim, flat. These were the ingredients compounded from a mixture of French painting and the relics of Aubrey Beardsley. *The Queen* did not want to have much to do with them except where it was not possible to resist. They still liked their painting to be strictly in the old tradition. 'Few of the moderns have arrived at a satisfactory solution to their problems. In the pursuit of truth, the abstract is a poor substitute for the concrete. Some go beyond the limits of our intelligibility, some wilfully seek ugliness. Others are bewildered by the multiplicity of contradictory doctrines and trying to swallow the whole fail to digest even a part. Besides, there is always a certain amount of leg pulling and stunting.' Of Modigliani the art critic said: 'These narrow necks, these prim and tightened mouths, these blank eyes emit an atmosphere of poverty of

Marguerite D'Alvarez as Delilah

Chaliapin in
The Barber of Seville

'*Miss Hermione Baddeley,
the clever little actress*'

*Yehudi Menuhin,
at the age of twelve after a recital
at the Albert Hall*

invention, stupidity and boredom, from which I fly.' When they did venture to encourage modern art they were atavistically amazed to find so much talent among the lower classes. 'Indeed, some of the most immature pictures, some of those which may be the work of pavement artists, plumbers or decorators of ice cream barrows, are not the least exciting or interesting.'

The theatre was lively. The young actors were astonishingly gifted —the paper devoted a regular page to their portraits—Edith Evans, Fay Compton, Gladys Cooper, Sybil Thorndyke, Gerald du Maurier and Ernest Thesiger. They were a powerful group. *The Queen* best liked drawing-room comedy. Shaw was still too risky for them. The first night of *St Joan* produced this notice: 'It may be because I saw *St Joan* on the second night that the delicious enthusiasm which has inflamed many other critics of Mr Shaw's play and Miss Thorndyke's performance did not touch me at all. There was not a single moment throughout the whole evening when the excitement of what was going on on the stage stilled all of the many coughs which exploded intermittently in the stalls.'

The young writers were also creating an entirely new vein. 'It has been suspected that Mr Aldous Huxley was weary of fiction and would presently retreat into realms of pure philosophy, where many of his delighted admirers could not follow him, but *Point Counterpoint*, his new work, is a long meaty novel. The writing is exquisite in its delicate integrity and the effect of the book is entirely moral, but Mr Huxley, in what one guesses to be a puritanical, well-controlled disgust at his puppets, is extremely outspoken. I doubt if the most modern mother of boys and girls will leave *Point Counterpoint* lying about, but she is deficient in consciousness of her own times if she does not read it herself.'

'Any sugary taste left by the sentimental novel of Mr Warwick Deeping will certainly disappear with a reading of Mr Evelyn Waugh's novel — the first novel of a clever writer. Mr Waugh himself says it is meant to be funny. It is also meant to be a little shocking; but it takes a lot to shock us nowadays. This illustrated novelette is certainly funny in parts; but farcical would be a truer description of it as a whole. There are, however, some shrewd touches of characterisation under the absurd portraits; and if Mr Waugh can discipline his riotous humour he may some day give us a really funny book. This one is mainly promise — and parody.' *The Queen* however really preferred Mr Beverley Nichols: 'That talented exploiter of his own youth, Mr Beverley Nichols, still appears to feel divinely young although it is now a year or two since he wrote his autobiographical *Twenty Five*. In a bunch of American impressions called The Star Spangled Manner, Mr Nichols scintillates with Gloria Swanson, stirs Professor Coolidge to profundity, and tries to explain the American woman's resort to clubs and "uplift" . . .' All in all, they were deliciously wide of the mark. This was the jazz age — its mentor was America — its heroes, Colette, Mistinguette, Wodehouse, Sacha Guitry, Mary Pickford, Valentino, Edith Sitwell. It was the day of fast cars, golf, films, cocktail parties, tennis parties, just parties, parties and dancing. *The Queen* could barely make a stand against it, 'It is no use fulminating against jazz. If people want jazz they will have it, and I believe that if we let it run its course (like any other disease) it will perish of its own apparent inanity.'

The Thirties

APRIL 22nd,
1937

The QUEEN

THE LADY'S NEWSPAPER

ONE
SHILLING

THE FIRST LADIES IN THE LAND

Is there no leader
who will call out the best in us,
show us the way to virtue?

Jazz did not die of its own inanity but much else did. The new formula for life, which the country had been searching for during the twenties, was forced upon society by circumstances rather than by choice. The 1930s were a period of disillusionment and growing apprehension which not even *The Queen*, with its ostrich capacity for glossing over manifestly unpalatable truths, could ignore. The domestic situation in Britain was worse than it had ever been, and was the more galling because the sacrifices which the upper classes had made, the concessions which had been extracted from them, the higher taxation, the new death duties — all appeared to have been in vain.

The new status of women which enabled them to go out to work looked rather sour when so many men were unemployed. The world situation which was to have been transformed by victory and the wise deliberations of the League of Nations, looked grim. It was a sorry story. After the national crisis of 1931 it seemed that there was no hope of any sort: 'The pessimists tell us to prepare for the worst; that the world depression has by no means reached its climax and that we have many anxious months possibly years ahead. They say that civilisation is a failure and that there is practically no hope left of any satisfactory solution to our problems.'

But let it not be supposed that the readers of *The Queen* would really allow such circumstances to affect their manner of living. 'The London Season is undoubtedly one of the seven wonders of the

modern world. People said it would never survive the war, that modern youth did not want set entertainments in the grand manner, dignity, tradition, but they were wrong, for here in 1931 the season is starting again to run its triumphant course through the summer.' All the old prejudices, all the old snobberies, all the complaints were still there. Servants as usual set the tone for their attitude: 'The social status of the servant is very largely to blame for the fact that though there is so much unemployment, young women refuse to enter our homes. Truly it is a ridiculous position. As long as homes exist we must have workers.' In a contradictory way, it was suggested at the height of the depression that every house should take on an extra servant to relieve unemployment. The paper began to recom-

Viscount Moore and Princess Aly Khan

mend foreign servants, though they thought that Mrs Sacheverell Sitwell was a little extreme in having a black Nanny for her children. Needless to say the domestic situation was not all that bad. It was still possible to worry about what a butler's duties might be if there were only one footman, or whether it were right that the kitchen maid should make tea for the Servants Hall when the parlour maid was out.

The new-found gentility of the twenties continued and was manifested in an aggrieved nostalgia. There was much talk of the good old days, much sighing over changes. In London, clubs were closing and Ranelagh, the favourite meeting place of Edwardian garden party society, was bought up by Ansbachers for building develop-

'The Countess Hauglitz-Reventlow with her son Lance. The Countess was formerly Miss Barbara Hutton'

ment. The development later failed, much to everyone's delight. Daly's theatre had to be shut down and many of London's largest houses disappeared in favour of large business premises. But Belgrave Square and Eaton Square were still the same as they had always been. The rich stayed rich while the poor got poorer. The atmosphere of smart opulence which they managed to maintain while unemployment figures rose makes it hard to believe that society was very much perturbed by the appalling conditions which more than half the population of the country had to endure. A breathless columnist was able to write: 'My dears — Eton and Harrow match, the Royal Garden Party, and now Cowes and Scotland and cures and things that people do who make the round of the seasons, depression or no depression.' A revival of political entertaining in 1936 was applauded. 'Traditions of ducal splendour are upheld by the tall, stately Duchess of Sutherland both at Hampden House and at Dunrobin. Aloof and beautiful, her plans for entertaining are seldom made public. She has wonderful jewels and knows how to wear them. She travels by car or in a private train. Lady Cowdray: This hostess's fleet of yellow cars is easily seen in Mayfair. The Liberal party claim her as a hostess . . . '

By the standards of the thirties, to be notorious was better than to be unknown, and to be talked about in the gossip columns better than to be ignored, not only for actresses but for debutantes as well. So general was this that the paper advised them against seeking publicity: 'Don't look longingly at the Press photographers. Don't come down the stairs of the Café de Paris as if you were a film star arriving at her own first night. Don't be nice to the gossip columnists. It is quite recent — this craving for publicity.' The arrogance of their snobbery was as tasteless as ever, enabling them to comment on two people in this fashion: 'The announcement that Mrs Barbara Wootton, the celebrated economist and educationalist, is to marry Mr George Wright, a Fulham taxi-cab driver, may seem strange at first sight, but they are an exceptional couple.'

In substance the lives of the rich were changed very little in the thirties from what they had been in the twenties. Nothing was taken away but a great deal was added. Their frolics persisted, but they were forced to become aware of much which they had previously ignored. This awareness changed their attitudes considerably. As early as 1932, *The Queen* was advocating reform of the divorce laws, much on the lines of A. P. Herbert's Act of 1937: 'So great are the anomalies of the present laws of divorce, so unjustly do they press on

'Two workers will finish the job in the fraction of the time of one . . .'

the innocent and so utterly absurd are they in many cases if carried out logically that men and women of the highest eminence and responsibility have long urged reform on behalf of true morality. Difficult divorce means easy separation, a dangerous legal arrangement which by giving freedom to neither party undoubtedly adds to the number of irregular unions and illegitimate children.'

The paper still clung to its deeply set notions of morality. 'Now comes the new morality which advocates the casting away of accepted ethical and social codes, established through man's struggle towards an ideal, which have on the whole been found to work. We find it is left to our century to preach as a duty the abandonment of some of our time-honoured beliefs. Fortunately the teaching of new history is confined at present to a few destructive spirits eager to destroy all that is old, the good and the bad alike, before being able to construct anything new which meets the needs of human beings who have souls as well as bodies.'

Frank parent-child sex discussions were encouraged by teachers and psychologists, and sex tended to take on a rather jolly and generally disinfectant aspect: 'As Sir Archibald Thompson expressed it in one of his marvellous lectures "Sex is the root whose flower is

*'Parents should see
that their daughters have opportunities
of meeting nice men . . .'*

love". When parents look on it from this angle they will be able to "Hitch the Sex Wagon to a Star" instead of, as is now the case, associating it with that which is undesirable.' Even the stranger aspects of sex came to be noticed. Boarding schools for girls, which had been so ardently championed for some years before, were suddenly a subject for concern. It was discovered that these schools fostered lesbianism. One girl committed suicide on account of her infatuation for a teacher and this incident, together with the German film *Mädchen in Uniform* and countless schoolgirl novels on the topic, gave rise to comment and correspondence. Parents wrote of girls' boarding schools as being dens of iniquity, and a headmistress wrote darkly of sex-starved teachers responding too ardently to the girls' emotions. The beneficial aspect of this flurry of alarm was the breaking down of barriers between boys and girls of school age. Another headmistress declared: 'From the age of 16 upwards I would myself rather see a girl enjoying a friendship with her brother's friends than falling madly in love with one of my staff.'

The freedom of discussion about sex was part of a new self-absorbed vanity which was typical of the decade. There are many

reasons to account for this particular manifestation. First, psychology became fashionable; secondly, girls were admired no longer for their virtues and spiritual qualities but more for their nubile attractions; and thirdly, youth was still at a premium and after ten years the glitter of the Bright Young Things was somewhat tarnished. The thirties were the age of face-lifting, electric stimulants, diets, lavish cosmetics, strict corsets and saucy brassières.

The craze for psychology, which was the chief aspect of this phenomenon, was only a part of the disillusionment and its attendant fears which made the people seek refuge in the comfort of a father figure.

The taste of the 1930s perhaps reflects the times more clearly than one would have expected. There was a note of austere severity — no pictures, no picture rails, no panelled doors, no moulding on ceilings. Even the Georgian era was thought to have a self-conscious primness, while the Victorians were despicable. Raymond Mortimer wrote: 'About a hundred years ago a mysterious malady of the eyes began to sweep the world. Houses, and everything in them, became uglier and uglier. This fact is now universally recognised, and almost everyone who can afford it has sold his or her grandfather's vast Victorian residence, with most of its contents, and bought a Georgian house, filling it with Chippendale, Sheraton, old china and eigh-

From a photographer's advertisement

teenth-century silver.' *The Queen* naturally represented the Conservative attitudes of its readers — the same ones we have seen all along. Whereas they noticed the general desire to get away from the stereotyped Victorian mahogany, red brocade wallpaper, and family portraits, they did not feel that a too ruthless attitude to the Victorians should be voiced.

In art they clung to their cherished Academicians, becoming almost savage at the thought of Epstein, and it took them until 1938 before they would admit the post-Impressionists to the ranks of the orthodox. Of writing their views were similar: 'Whatever one's opinions may be of the various poets who have contributed to *New Signatures*, the volume is interesting as indicating the thoughts, moods and ideas of the younger generation. But I cannot see of what value are Mr Michael Roberts's introductory remarks. He tells us that "new knowledge and new circumstances have compelled us to think and feel in ways not expressible in the old language at all". Yet Mr Julian Bell finds the eighteenth-century couplet quite adequate to express all he wishes to say.' They spoke of the gloomy plays by Elmer Rice, the formless and plotless novels of the young contemporary novelists. J. B. Priestley was the man for them: 'As a novelist Mr J. B. Priestley possesses three qualities any one of which I fear is fatal to his chances of being taken seriously by the pontifical critics for whom fiction's only function is the dissection of diseased and

Greta Garbo in Anna Karenina, *a painting by Robert D. Greenham*

J. B. Priestley

'A new portrait of Elinor Glyn, with two feline friends'

Mr A. A. Milne with his son Christopher Robin

decadent minds. For Mr Priestley clearly believes that a novel should entertain, should tell a coherent story and should deal with ordinary men and women.' In an article on the writers who were likely to survive, *The Queen* chose Kipling, Barrie, Shaw, Wells, William Watson, A. E. Housman, and E. M. Forster as almost certainties. Among the possibles were Virginia Woolf (but her art was too difficult for the ordinary intelligent reader) Sheila Kaye Smith, W. W. Jacobs, Aldous Huxley and Sean O'Casey. Their doubtful cases were perhaps more accurate — A. A. Milne (whom they thoughtlessly compared with Lewis Carroll), the Sitwells (all clever and original but lacking in something vital) and Noel Coward.

The cinema rose in prestige. In the twenties cinemagoers had mostly consisted of servant girls and the lower classes. Fortunately

George Bernard Shaw, Wendy Hiller, Leslie Howard and Anthony Asquith at the time of the film of Pygmalion

the Royal Family installed a private cinema at Sandringham, which example made such popular idols as Greta Garbo, Marlene Dietrich and Robert Taylor available to people of all classes. There were hazards, however, to this new medium: 'The development of the wireless and the cinema which enables the whole civilised world to hear and see practically the same things has led to a growing similarity of taste, outlook and feeling, which should be counterbalanced by the encouragement of individuality in the young. This similarity of feeling, if not directed to a very high ideal, may evolve into the herd spirit reducing the individual to an automaton — a mere cog in the machine.' 'In *Enemies of the Public*, we are shown the actual evolution of the gangster. Why — and this is not written with mock piety — we cannot be given some wholesome entertainment must bewilder all self-respecting cinemagoers. Indeed it is no exaggeration to say that films of the type just mentioned are a serious menace and will

Gloria Swanson
in Tonight or Never
at the Tivoli, London

Tommy and Gracie Fields
in Walk this Way
at the Winter Garden Theatre

Gordon Harker in The Frog

Mrs Stanley Baldwin
and Lady Irwin
at the opening of Parliament

surely breed a race of desperadoes within our own shores unless a strict censorship of our undesirable and evil influencing films is exercised.'

At the theatre, *The Queen* admired Ivor Novello and Noel Coward. These two outshone any more adventurous playwrights.

Again it is clear that the social life of the upper classes was maintained on pretty much the same scale as it had been in the twenties, but a greater awareness of politics was forced upon them by events both at home and abroad. Unemployment was something which could hardly be ignored. The home fit for heroes had failed and only the very secure could afford to remain untroubled by the economic and social disturbances. In 1933 just under three million people were unemployed, and at least a quarter of a million were living below

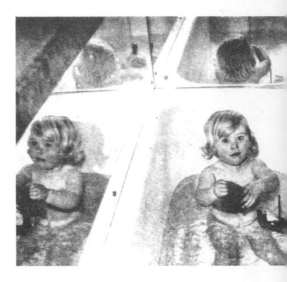

*The present Lady Lewisham
when she was
Miss Raine McCorquodale (1932)*

*Queen Maud of Norway
among the Pearly Queens*

the poverty line. *The Queen* estimated as late as 1936 that only fifty per cent of the population could afford a diet sufficient to maintain their health. This was more than even the readers of the paper could bear. Lady Melchett wrote: 'It is a very sad thing to realise that there are thousands of children in the distressed areas who are not getting enough to eat.' It was after all distressing that people should die of hunger. While their own standard of living was unaffected, an interesting change came over the thinking of the rich. First of all a fear of riots and revolution gave some impetus to their natural humanitarian zeal: 'Every workless man may be a menace to the country, every employed man an asset . . . ' Secondly they felt that they had been deprived by taxation and other privations of that pious charity which used to be their perquisite. The resentment which they felt at finding that the poor, deprived of their munificence, became poorer despite the promises of the State, prompted a strange anomaly. In their indignation at the failure of the Government to fulfil the duty which it had wrenched from them, they embraced a totally foreign, socialist idea which was to lead to the foundation of the Welfare State. They seriously wished conditions to be better, and believed they would have been if the old regime remained. As power

The wedding of
Miss Laura Bonham-Carter and
Mr Joseph Grimond (1938)

had passed from them, they were determined that the new pretenders should be forced to perform their functions properly.

They were still reluctant to give up entirely their paternal status: 'The State must, of course, do a large share in relieving the unemployed, but when it has done all it can — it has by no means done this as yet — there still remains much for the voluntary worker to do.' For the first time also came the realisation that it was the social structure itself which was at fault. The Dean of St Paul's wrote for the paper: 'This Empire Thanksgiving will not be properly observed if it does not stimulate us to feel more keenly our responsibility for those imperfections in our social order which make the boon of freedom for some of our fellow citizens little more than a mockery.' It was a great disillusionment — so much had been sacrificed for no return.

Nothing seemed to have worked out as it had been expected. The women of the thirties began to react against the triumphant feminism of the twenties. Girls instead of persisting in wishing for a career, began again to say that they hoped to marry. The reasons for this were twofold. First the shortage of jobs for men, secondly the prizes of emancipation turned out to be not so glamorous as they had seemed in prospect. 'This glorious freedom; how much of it did we really need? What have we gained in addition? The privilege of doing men's chores and our own as well, but without being thanked for it this time. We have the privilege of earning our living, because having swamped out the almost overloaded male employment market, men can no longer find the work which would enable them to keep us. We have the privilege of dragging out day after day, by train, tram and bus, to do the work of men, to return and spend our leisure hours mending, washing and ironing as we have always done, since men have not thoughtfully adapted themselves to do these things for us in their own turn.'

There was little comfort at home. Juvenile delinquency was spreading. Religion held no interest for the young. The youth of England was more serious than it had been in the twenties. They were said to be more interested in politics and their work and less concerned with sex and personal problems than ever before, but they were still floundering. 'One young woman summed up the attitude of her generation to me the other night declaring that it was a general feeling among her contemporaries. "We are sick and tired of drifting. We want discipline for our children, discipline *and* discipline AND discipline!" That she is right is shown in the main

Lord and Lady Birkenhead
with Lady Gomer Berry
at the wedding of Lady Pamela Smith
and the Hon. Michael Berry

by the success of such highly disciplined movements as the Young Fascists and Young Communists. A reaction from the often aimless and abortive revolutionary ardours of the past few years.'

The need for an authority to respect was great. The traditional repository for such emotions, the one symbol which might have helped was to fail them utterly. The Crown, which had for the past twenty years been becoming more and more the source of sentimental strength, succumbed to human weakness.

In November 1935, *The Queen* wrote: 'Happy for himself, thrice happy for his country have been the Prince's bachelor years, but should he ever decide to change his present honourable estate for that of holy matrimony there would descend upon him a flood of

goodwill from every corner of the world.' The matrimony which King Edward chose was not sufficiently holy for his constitutional advisers.

In the matter of the abdication, *The Queen* kept as stiff an upper lip as even its most proper readers could wish for. The front page of the issue of 10 December 1936 showed a photograph of the King, the Duke and Duchess of York, Queen Mary, Baldwin and Lord Halifax. Underneath was written: 'The people of the Empire have, during the past week, been watching with sympathetic eyes, the enactment of one of the most significant dramas in our constitutional history.' Most of the rest of the issue was about the approaching Coronation, having been prepared before the crisis arose.

*The Lying-in-State of King George V
and the funeral procession;
King Edward VIII and his three brothers*

King Edward VIII

Mrs Simpson

King George VI

The issue of 17 December, after the abdication speech, showed on the cover the new King and Queen, and beneath it the words 'God Bless Their Majesties'. Apart from a statement that all Royal engagements had been cancelled, there was no mention of the abdication, nor of the Duke of Windsor nor of Mrs Simpson. The Coronation was discussed quite happily, as though there had been no change in the dramatis personae. Loyal greetings were extended to the new Monarch: 'Our first word of greeting to the new King and Queen who have so recently ascended the Throne must be, in the name of all our readers, one of affectionate and heartfelt good wishes . . . They now stand as the embodiment of this realm and its centuries of great traditions. There is no one of this age but must be

glad; the more so that beside our King, of the House of Windsor, there stands a lady of British blood who in her own person has linked the Crown with the people of this realm.' This was presumably intended to mean that the country was lucky not to have Mrs Simpson. It was only the second time she had been referred to, even obliquely, although in various photographs of the King one sees a feminine foot or hand or corner of a skirt belonging to someone clumsily excised. The first occasion was a photograph of her which appeared in 1935 in conjunction with an article attacking American women: 'Modern American women demand money over and above all things else in the world. Each wants to be better dressed, smarter in appearance and to have more admirers than her neighbours, and these desires require money and yet more money . . . They treat their husbands as slaves, or money-making machines. The pleasures of the American woman also require much money. Most of her delights take the form of snobbery. She must live in the most expensive apartment, entertain lavishly and feel that her social position is growing more high and unassailable every day.' By the time the Coronation came, the English, with their singular adaptability, had managed to transfer to the new King all the loyalty which they had felt for the old one. But the situation had added to the general sense of insecurity.

The greatest disappointment in an age of disillusion was the final realisation that the Great War with all its casualties had been fought for no purpose. On the anniversary of the Armistice in 1937, *The Queen* declared that the high hopes of 1918 seemed faded and dead: 'The mood of the nation is a mood of disillusion. Very far we seem now from the moment of infinite relief and sudden enthusiasm when the guns ceased fire and the survivors turned eagerly to the future in the expectation that a renewal of life awaited them. An era of universal peace appeared not only the reward they had earned but the necessary application of a lesson so terrible that mankind could never forget it. Yet today once more the world is resonant with wars, and murmurous with rumours of wars. Peace came with perpetration of hate and not the beginning of reconciliation; and so the great ideal for which so many lives were given evades the grasp of humanity.'

The despair which was felt as Europe rolled inexorably towards another war, was gradual in coming. The League of Nations was the foundation stone upon which all post-war ideals had been built. Its history, from its enthusiastic creation until it declined into pure farce after Italy's invasion of Abyssinia, corresponded exactly to the mood

*Amelia Earhart
Her last flight*

DECEMBER 25th,
1935

The QUEEN

ONE
SHILLING

THE LADY'S NEWSPAPER

of the country. During the twenties the League did not have to stand any particularly severe test. It was not until the Japanese invasion of Manchuria that anyone could really judge whether international arbitration would prove to be a panacea for world problems.

The League failed with the Japanese, but even in 1935 there was still hope that the Geneva Conference might avert the Abyssinian crisis: 'Having seen the League at work in all its departments one does sincerely feel that here is something which will endure, whose very existence is a recognition of world co-operation, an ideal to be struggled for through all difficulties, without which the alternative is chaos.' It is not until the Conference was well under way that it suddenly dawned upon the people that in such a situation the Covenant of 1919 bound them to enforce the sanctions with all their apparently inevitable implications: 'There are few in this country who do not deplore the necessity for this particular instance of united action. But what was the alternative? Only one which would have destroyed the last remnants of its attempts to build up a new world order based on the mutual respect for international obligations.' Had the sanctions been fully enforced the results might have been disastrous, but at least the League would not have been reduced to the complete mockery which resulted when it was finally agreed only to enforce a series of petty sanctions and without the all important one of oil. Even *The Queen*, usually unwilling to criticise any form of government action, described Hoare's policy as indefensible as promising the spoils to the aggressor. So by the end of October the British looked despondently at the League: 'Signor Mussolini's reliance on the incapability of the League (*vide* its handling of the Sino-Japanese trouble) was truly built on a firm foundation.'

The

QUEEN

July 19th, 1939.   ONE SHILLING

Faith in the League and the new-found ideals had led to an almost incomprehensible self deception about the possibility of war. At each crisis, *The Queen* pontificated with a bland optimism. 'Although Italian troops have been shipped to Africa, it is improbable that the nation would really wish an armed conflict with Abyssinia, possibly Mussolini himself least of all.' In the same year the paper commented on Germany: 'In the present situation moderation must be the watchword and extreme language must be avoided. If this course is followed, Germany, seeing the solidarity of world opinion, may yet return to the League and ask for the revision of the treaties in a peaceful and acceptable fashion.' In the anxiety to placate Germany, Britain was cast in the mythical role of the stabiliser of Europe. This self deception was the outcome of a general hatred and terror of war. Gone for ever was the war fever of the Edwardians. They no longer saw it as a glorious enterprise, but swung almost too far in blaming big business and war profiteers for the Great War. Beverley Nichols's book *Cry Havoc!*, published in 1933, was received with acclaim; 'Every word of *Cry Havoc!* is worth reading both for the astounding facts that are revealed, and the author's own reactions to the war problem . . . One is horrified to learn how the Comité des Forges, that sinister association of French ironmasters, helped to prolong the war. Such facts as these are ample proof that war is mostly a commercial proposition in which mighty business corporations are willing to kill and mutilate their fellow beings in an effort to obtain big dividends. Politicians of a certain class are dominated by armament firms; public schools teach war as a matter of course; the whole country is educated to believe in war. *Cry Havoc!* is an attempt to show the public how it is being gulled by unscrupulous place seekers and money barons . . . '

Peace at any price was the message the country wanted to hear, and in Chamberlain they found the man prepared to give it to them. At the time of the Sudetenland crisis *The Queen* commented: 'Had Mr Chamberlain refused Hitler's demands in so many words we would now be in the midst of a European conflagration. If you are in favour of peace, then Mr Chamberlain's efforts deserve your unstinted admiration.'

The attitude to European affairs was dismal. It contained both the old attitudes of indifference and a new-found weakness born of fear. The observations on the Spanish civil war recall precisely those made about the Franco-Prussian war: 'It is hard to imagine this Spanish Ilfracombe crowded with refugees and threatened with a siege. In

peaceful times, it is such a gay holiday town! With its golden sands, white villas and hydrangeas it is the last place one would associate with war.' The significance of the conflict being enacted there escaped them. All that mattered was that they were being deprived of a good place for a holiday. In September 1938, the end of the war was brought to their notice by the fact that Biarritz was enjoying its first good season since the Spanish trouble began.

Germany and Italy were differently treated, for anyone could see that these two countries were in a position to menace peace, but there was an obstinate refusal to see that not only were they in a position to do so but were actually doing so.

The thin quality of victory had so drained the national confidence that Britain floundered rudderless. It was noticeable that while there came from Europe a flood of propaganda, England had no reply. It was not only the will to proclaim their beliefs which seemed to be lacking, but also the faith that their beliefs were the right ones. In their dissatisfaction with the democracy which had evolved, they looked a little enviously at the two dictators of Germany and Italy. As young people wanted discipline so the whole country wanted it.

It is surprising how often excuses were found for Hitler. Persecution of the Jews was dismissed as unreal, and was claimed to be Germany's own domestic problem. There were attempts to laugh it off as ridiculous or even humorous. A great joke was made of Hitler's decree that shops should only be allowed to sell dolls with Aryan features. Even when the extent of the persecution became clear, there was no readiness to acknowledge that all could be as bad as it looked. 'Hitler's anti-Semitic tendency knew no bounds and the lot of Jews in Germany became almost unendurable. This was followed by the president's campaign against Roman Catholics and certain branches of the Lutheran Church. Trade Unions were abolished and Freemasonry almost destroyed. This is the dark side of the picture, but much good had resulted from his regime and it is too early and would be unfair to pronounce judgement on his works.' In the correspondence columns Hitler was occasionally attacked by readers: 'When citizens are arrested at will the country cannot be described as safe. When the population is terror stricken, the peace that rules is not worth the name . . . Your correspondent is apparently more concerned about the peace and order than about freedom and tolerance. As far as the question of atrocities is concerned and the general mutilation of the lives of those people who are not in accord with the Nazi regime, I only state briefly that I am prepared to

*'A very great Englishman
and his wife,
Mr and Mrs Neville Chamberlain'*

provide overwhelming evidence whenever called upon to do so.'

Mussolini was treated with the same consideration. Just before the Abyssinian invasion, *The Queen* claimed to know his mind better than he himself. 'In spite of the Duce's reiteration of his determination that he will not move from his former position we are certain he has in the back of his mind some conciliatory reservations.' On being proved wrong *The Queen* estimated that in the matter of the Abyssinian invasion Mussolini's efforts were undoubtedly beneficial, and adding winningly that, apart from his desire for power, there was nothing self-seeking about him. He was nominated in 1933 as one of the current personalities likely to become an Immortal, along with the Prince of Wales, Charlie Chaplin and the Chief Scout.

Hitler and Mussolini shared a quality irresistible to the English as these two quotations show. First a letter to the Editor about Hitler: 'Madam, there are two worlds, the moral or spiritual world and the material. No matter whether Herr Hitler has or has not to his credit actions in the material world unacceptable to our smug British ideas, he is ascending to heights far above ours in other things. Let me refer to one, the putting down of ill treatment of dumb animals. From what I have read, cruelty to our four-footed creatures is met with some punishment. Vivisection which is rampant in England and the Dominions, owing to the gullibility of the public and the callous minds of men of affairs, is now to be prohibited in Germany and Prussia. No, these things count for far more than do any of the objections against Hitler.' Secondly a leader about Mussolini: 'Mussolini first came into the daily consciousness of a great many people in this country by a gesture of simple humanity. We had not felt his influence in our daily lives, not troubled to think about his activities in Italy — and then he made Capri a sanctuary for birds . . . From that moment his name was uttered affectionately by thousands who had never thought of it before. He became to us a living force, liberating to our isle a myriad sweet-voiced messengers who but for him had struggled in trappers' nets, and ended their winged destiny on toast in French restaurants. And now he has come to our consciousness again in the matter of international peace. There will be more lives saved now, human lives, which we are pleased to think more important than those of birds. God knows if we are right . . . but wives and mothers will be glad of Mussolini.'

Where then were the British to find a father figure who would look after their destinies and those of their dumb friends? They chose Chamberlain. Other politicians were easily dismissed: 'More

'H. E. Benito Mussolini, dictator of Italy'

rumours of a new party in England — a party to form around Mr Eden, Mr Duff Cooper and Mr Churchill. I would not worry much about that. Mr Churchill is a wonderful speaker, especially in opposition, he is grand at general invective. Few statesmen have escaped the lash of his tongue. Anthony Eden is not like Winston. He lisps in sorrow rather than anger and I prophesy that he will not stray far from the fold. Mr Duff Cooper does not interest me at all.'

'Herr Adolf Hitler, President and Chancellor of the German Reich'

*March of the
Nazi Labour Corps
in Nuremberg*

Chamberlain they saw as a strong man, a man of oak, and so he was constantly presented and described. At the time of Munich he was seen as a fine representative of the British Lion: 'The theme of a thousand Nazi and Fascist ovations has been that the democracies are bankrupt for lack of discipline, and the future belongs only to a country that can submit themselves to a leader. Herr Hitler saw, in the oaken character of the man before him, that a free people in time of need can put forward a more effective leader than any of them, and can follow him with a loyalty that needs no external trappings.'

Munich seemed to prove to the appeasers that they had been right. In the next ten months, however, the rest of Czechoslovakia had been swallowed up and Poland was now threatened. But illusions were fostered in the face of any disaster. After a speech by Lord Halifax in July 1939 the political correspondent said: 'Our great worry during the September crisis was that we were not in a position to use such language. But thank God that has changed. They say in the United States the Lion roars again.' It had not been plain in September that that was what anyone was worried about.

Right up to the actual declaration of war *The Queen* tried to believe that it could not happen. In the middle of July they wrote of their expectations that Danzig would be settled easily. In August they pointed out that the Axis had no oil and therefore could not embark on a war. Two weeks before the outbreak: 'There is no sense in thinking that a settlement on peaceful lines is beyond the bounds of possibility.' It was pointed out that Italy had nothing to gain from a war and, without Italy, Germany could not undertake one. England had never been so well prepared. But war came. The dictators behaved like dictators after all, and not like well-bred Englishmen.

England responded as she should. Regret was expressed that the King and Queen had had their much-needed summer holiday upset for the second year in succession. Then the British got to work. 'There is a determination abroad, which I have never seen before, to finish this rascal, Hitler, off for good and all.'

Driving down the course at Ascot

The Second World War

The QUEEN

THE LADY'S NEWSPAPER & COURT CHRONICLE

Established 1861

Volume 186. No. 4853

Wednesday, December 27th, 1939

AIR CHIEF MARSHAL HIS MAJESTY THE KING

The danger is now at our own doors.
We have been accustomed to fight our battles on foreign soil,
but that is out of date.

The outbreak of war was almost a relief. Nerves had been tattered
by the long suspense. War meant that at last there was something
concrete to be done. All the malaise of the thirties was dispelled by
the common cause. The Great War had come as a surprise, this one
amazed nobody; but the external response was in some ways similar
to that of 1914. Patriotism was resurgent. Before the First War it had
been a disease. Now, although there were flickers of absurdity about
it, it represented more a feeling that here was a chance to do properly
a job which had been mishandled once and to eradicate the disgrace
of appeasement: 'What we have to set out to do is to rid Europe of a
madman who seeks to dominate the world, to teach Hitler as we
taught Napoleon that no man is big enough to be master of the world.'

England was once again in the position to cure the ills of the world.
There was no doubt in anyone's mind that she would do it: 'The
Royal Navy has already got a stranglehold on Germany. As I
suggested some weeks ago Germany has outrun her supplies of
materials and food. A lady who listened to the Danzig speech said,
"Hitler sounded like a rat in a trap". That is what he is.' They were
going to hang Hitler and their washing on the Siegfried Line, but
no one had really calculated for a moment how this brave nonsense
was to be accomplished.

The British Expeditionary Force with its obsolete guns and puttees
set off for France, while people at home knitted balaclavas and body-
belts for the trenches. This time they thought they were ready for it:

'There is a very vast difference between the early days of the Great War and the early days of this one so far as the public is concerned. Everything has been arranged by the Government. Food, transport, evacuation, radio, blackout and the rest had been considered and merely had to be put into operation.' 'England has been transformed into one great garrison camp . . . It does not cause one to lift an eyebrow to see gasmasks parked in the entrance halls of your friends' houses, nor does it surprise you to find your smartest girl friend driving a lorry.'

State visit of the French President Le Brun

While it was not possible to imagine what the scientific advances of the years between the wars would mean, there was a very real terror of bombardment: 'Those with large enough houses might do well to prepare for taking in people whose houses have been bombed. This sounds an extreme eventuality, but in the present state of tragic lunacy nothing is too fantastic to consider.'

But for many months nothing happened. 'All the fears people had at the beginning of the war seem to have gone from their minds and they have now settled down so philosophically to this state of war. Food is plentiful and the butter ration seems adequate—we are only concluding that we made pigs of ourselves before the war. Many people are back in London, and except for empty streets with scarcely any traffic in them it has changed very little. Indoors nothing is different (except for more permanent looking black curtains) and the restaurants are even more gay than before. Theatres too are doing very well.' The early days of 1940 were marked only by fretful inactivity: 'Our B.E.F. in France are not so badly off for comfort but they and the commanders have a different problem, namely Boredom. One imagines these young men will welcome a scrap instead of the everlasting report "Nothing doing on the Western Front".'

There was talk of peace in the spring, and the period of waiting gave rise to the perennial grumbles that normal activities should be so sadly interrupted. The weather was perfect for winter sports—it was a pity not to go ski-ing. 'The powers-that-be have seen fit in their wisdom to place the veto on the holding of point-to-points. This is an attitude of mind which I find hard to reconcile with the true facts,

The Countess of Rosse

*Fay Compton as Queen Victoria
and John Gielgud as Disraeli*

Sentry at the Houses of Parliament

Coastal Defences at Dover

it seems to me to be as selfish and one-sided as it is unjust in its conception.' But, as in the Great War, the rich contrived to find some pleasure: 'A little ray of sunshine! The French Riviera is to open up for the winter. Paris is lighted up and fairly bright by day. Now the Riviera is hoping to return to business as usual.' The Boche appeared reluctant to fight.

Chamberlain was still Prime Minister. Churchill was regarded rather as a nuisance, interfering in matters that were not his business: 'At the Mansion House Mr Churchill had yet another smack at Norway for being a one-sided neutral, so that Mr Chamberlain has to apply the balm to it. What good does it do? Anyway it is hardly his pigeon. How would he like Lord Halifax to discuss Scapa Flow in public?' Churchill's history was almost unforgivable, by the standards of the ruling classes. His voice was a classless one, not appreciated by privilege. May 1940 saw a change. Chamberlain was altogether too cautious, too fearful of positive action to be England's leader in war. In the third week of that month Churchill took over: 'We are unanimous in our choice and in the belief that Mr Churchill is the right man for the emergency. He is what Jackie Fisher would have called bloody minded.'

Feeding bombed-out children

*Children painting curbs
for the black-out*

*The Duchess of Gloucester
at an Invalid kitchen during the blitz*

Defeat in France was incisive and brutal. The battered fragments
of the British Expeditionary Force were precariously rescued from
Dunkirk. Morale in the face of disaster was perversely high. Everyone
felt he might have a chance to fight a German. A conversation between a foreigner and an English woman was reported:

'"When I was in England in the last war, women would pretend
to be gay, yet you could see they were unhappy. Yet *you*—when the
war is come to the very shores of England—you are all so calm, you
look so *well*! Almost as though you find life good. How do you
explain this?"'

'"Don't you see that we as women are thankful that we are not
pushed into a backwater—that we are in the war too? There is a
fever about—a fever to get the Hun and push him into the sea;
drown his bombast, his pomp and his beastliness forever. We might
hurt him—draw his blood—it would be Heaven!"'

Rationing became drastic. Everyone gathered old pots and pans,
iron railings—anything to make munitions. Slogans waged a war on
waste. 'Don't let the Squander Bug Get You'; 'Crusts are precious';
'Not more than five inches of water in *my* bath, Mummy.' And the
King had a black line drawn round his tub, so that he should not use
too much hot water and waste fuel. No longer was there any
grumbling about the lack of parties. It was amusing and also a little
brave of the wives, without cook or maids, to produce stews of dried
egg, bacon rind, snoek, spam or whatever happened to be the fad
of the moment.

*School competition:
a child's poster for
National Savings*

Enjoying all this, the upper classes were inclined to overestimate the working man's patriotic instinct: 'Chancellors and Ministers of State and high officers of the Treasury have queer notions about the working man. Income tax on small wages they consider impossible. But is it? When in the last war a whole new class was brought into the income-tax field, a thousand whom I knew quite well received the blue papers with highest satisfaction. "We are now income-tax payers", they explained joyfully. The working man *wants* to do his bit.' A few weeks later the miners refused to work more than a four day week, saying the fifth day's pay would just go to the Government. In this war, class consciousness received a final blow. It was not, as in the Great War, that the rich tried temporarily to find common ground with all classes—this time it was completely natural. Privileged life was palpably impossible. No one questioned the taking over of large houses. Rationed clothes could not be that much smarter than average. The anonymity of a uniform brought everyone closer together. Everybody had to eat the same things even if they were prepared to pay a large house charge, say at the Savoy, over and above the five-shilling limit placed on the price of any meal. There was a very definite feeling that anyone might be killed the next day which also led to social barriers appearing less important, certainly to the young people. 'The debutante of the past had a season in order to meet eligible young men, the standard of eligibility being set by her parents; the debutante of today drives up to London with a young man who is stationed nearby, while at home her mother says wearily that Robin *seems* quite a nice young man, and wishes she knew what his surname was.' Above all the bombing, with all its attendant camaraderie and gallantry, eradicated finally the possibility of believing that the working classes were a different species.

This relaxation did not mean that all the charms of privilege were forgotten. 'What is to become of the stately homes of England; the castles and mansions of the country and the houses in town? I believe that the old families will hold tenaciously to those homes which link them with the soil of England.' Servants were of course expected to recognise the advantages which were open to them: 'How foolish is the rebellion against wearing a uniform. And what about the use of the word servant, how small minded to reject it! Surely no worthwhile woman wants to sit in a Cinema or roam the streets every night.'

Mrs Roosevelt in London

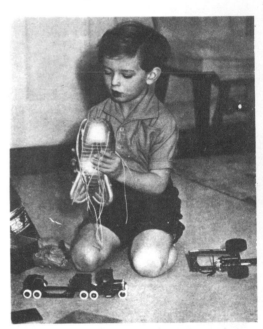

The Duke of Kent,
died on active service 1942

Prince Edward of Kent

As the war progressed the inestimable qualities of the upper classes were claimed to be largely responsible for any victory. 'Happily the titled classes and landed gentry have in this war, as in conflicts in the past, responded ungrudgingly to the call of their country and added new lustre to their family records proving the truth of the old saying blood will tell, and by their example and qualities of leadership have largely contributed to bringing victory within our grasp.' The skill of the Battle of Britain pilots was attributed to

The Hi Gang.
In front: Vic Oliver,
Bebe Daniels, Ben Lyon;
behind: Jay Wilbur,
Sam Browne, Harry S. Pepper

Augustus John buying
a charity raffle ticket from
the daughter of the Argentine Ambassador
—the prize being a lemon

their sporting training: 'Our pilots are second to none, their courage and hardihood unequalled. Some of these qualities come from the hunting field for in the piping days of peace few went harder and better than the members of the R.A.F.' When a considerable number of Japanese aircraft were brought down over the Pacific it was explained that they had not the skill which could be learned out hunting. They did not have what hunting men call good hands.

That the emancipation of women was complete became plain very early. Their contribution was expected of them just as much as it was expected of men. They were important and so did not assume the deliberate dowdiness which women in the first war had adopted to show they were doing their bit. 'Night time beauty is one of the new problems which present circumstances impose upon the well-groomed woman. Will you go to the shelter in full war paint wilfully neglecting the advice of most beauty specialists, or do you intend to rank among those strong-minded creatures who follow their bedtime rules to beauty and appear among their fellow shelterers literally besmeared with skin food?'

The war progressed, with the help of advice from *The Queen*. 'Some time ago the Russians made the experiment of carrying troops by aeroplane and dropping them by parachute. Even grown up people can be found to believe it possible in war. The idea is just silly. The parachute is only possible for an adventurous spy.' The bombing of

Fashions for the air-raid shelter

Private Phillips Price, M.P.
and Private Leslie Boyce, M.P.,
High Sheriff of Gloucester,
in the Home Guard

Nurses attached to the
Free French Forces

London led to the repetition of the wild hatred which was felt for the Germans in the First World War: 'Nothing I imagine has so effectively stiffened our resistance to the Nazi attack on London as the repeated onslaughts on Buckingham Palace. Their Majesties were a little surprised at the deliberate attacks on the Palace but seemed outwardly little disturbed.' This feeling, in fact, seemed at times almost stronger than it had been in the Great War. 'It was quite refreshing to have Mr Richard Law recommend the application of the hangman's noose to the neck of Hermann Goering and the rest of the loathsome Nazi crew.' 'The Archbishop of York has no illusions to their character and the atrocities they committed . . . As to Hitler, Himmler and their gang he would outlaw them and allow the first person who caught them to shoot each and everyone without trial. It is good to hear an Archbishop talking sound sense which the ordinary person can understand.'

It was the Germans who were hated, not the Italians. It was somehow believed that the Italians had not wanted to fight and had been led astray by bad leaders. 'Not for one generation but for many, the word German will be a term of abomination and loathing throughout the civilised world. The German name will be regarded not only with hatred but with horror. The German people have sunk to a grade lower than the standards of mankind.' Good treatment was recommended for the Italian prisoners: 'they may be

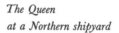

*The Queen
at a Northern shipyard*

*The King and Queen
looking at the bomb damage
at Buckingham Palace*

grateful—the Hun would not. He would not understand. The better he is treated the more arrogant he becomes. He is always a Hun.'

It was not only the enemy who came in for vituperation. Our Allies too were tiresome. As far as Russia was concerned, this was not surprising. It needed a lot to get over Russia's pact with Germany just before the War. English Communists had been loathed as traitors: 'It is very encouraging to learn that the Home Secretary is now taking real action against the Communists. I drew attention only a few weeks ago . . . to the subversive activities of these people . . . I often wonder why it is that professors and what are known as

intellectuals line themselves with such a movement.' Even after Hitler's betrayal of Russia, and Russia had become an ally, our own Communists were felt to be untrustworthy. There had to be a change in order to maintain good relations with Russia. One more perspicacious writer pointed out: 'Stalin . . . is not fighting for us. He fights only for Russia. For us he does not care one iota.' But later the theme was changed: 'Russia looks like winning the race to Berlin. It does not really matter which of us gets there first so long as all three do get there and are of one mind when they arrive. The Red Army will be an excellent advance agent.'

Charlie Chaplin

Sir Arthur Harris,
Chief of Bomber Command,
at the Red Army Day reception
in the Soviet Embassy

The Americans were scorned more than the Russians by the readers of *The Queen*. Throughout the war the United States was a source of irritation. She was too slow coming in, and did not seem to be expressing anything more useful than good wishes. When the American Army came over in 1942 there was much to resent. There were reminders that the American forces had come to fight for England, but the British felt that they had already borne the brunt of the battle and were thereby reduced to a state of impoverished chaos and that really the Americans should be grateful. The Americans arrived looking confident and agreeably laden with chewing-gum, cigarettes, and stockings made from some new stuff called nylon. At first there were efforts to understand them: 'To British people familiarity is effrontery; to Americans it is friendliness. To understand the American's outlook you must understand the fundamental keynote of his character is gregariousness. You never see him alone.

General de Gaulle and Cardinal Hinsley

Montgomery and Eisenhower shortly before D-day

Conference at Teheran. Stalin, Roosevelt, Churchill; behind: Molotov, Sarah Churchill, Eden

When you walk down Piccadilly at night you find him in droves, clustered round lamp posts, leaning up against buildings, bunched in doorways. Many mothers regard this as an example of licentious soldiery but the truth of the matter is that hanging around on street corners is an old American custom. The advances he makes are also customary. That taxi-cab pass is not regarded as an impertinence but as a compliment.'

In 1942 this was the attitude: 'We are so grateful to you for coming. I hope we in England will often remember to say this. For these men have given up their careers, left their secure homes in the Middle West and come a very long way to do a very great job. They are deadly serious and mean business, are not out for entertainment or a good time but we owe them that kind of understanding recognition.' By 1944 a more typical comment was: 'Newspapers persist in talking about how much we owe America because we received destroyers, guns and planes to fight a battle that is at least as much America's battle as ours, let British newspapers ask how much America owes us for the lives of our men fighting in nominally American armies.'

Americans were not content with winning girls away from young British soldiers — they claimed to have won the whole war. When, in 1945, Errol Flynn almost single handed triumphed in the Burma Campaign at the Plaza Cinema, anti-American feeling reached fever pitch — the more so as the film happened to coincide with the publication of our War Debt to the United States.

From steel helmets to straw hats

Sightseeing tour of London for American troops

'*Hugh, Earl of Lonsdale,
typical of the very best in
British sportsmanship*'

Racing at Newbury

Derby Day

As victory came closer, the privileged classes began to look with a certain alarm at what the post-war years might bring. At the beginning of the war there had been the strong reaction against class consciousness, and a general spirit of good will engendered by unity against the enemy. There was a genuine desire that the men who were fighting so bravely should not be betrayed on their return. 'Little birds swoop down and hiss into our ears the most exciting news about wonderful plans for Reconstruction after the war, and how every man will have his home, his job and reasonable leisure. We already know quite a lot about pre-fabricated houses and how Mr Butler intends to see that in future we shall be a wholly educated, instead of a half-educated nation as we are at the present. We are informed that our men will come back from the wars to a promise realised, and not, like last time, to a land in which ex-Servicemen had to pawn their war medals in order to achieve the barest sustenance of life.' Even towards the end there was a realisation that some of the lessons of war should not be forgotten: 'In wartime Britain a somewhat sparse diet has been divided fairly throughout the nation . . . Unless the sharing and unity of wartime be carried over into peace, there will be no effective human will to preserve peace. We shall be at the mercy of the next bandits who make use of the next wave of discouragement and cynicism.'

Lord and Lady Louis Mountbatten

Mr Randolph Churchill marries Miss Pamela Digby

There isn't even half an engine to spare for unnecessary journeys

.. so 'stay put' this summer

RAILWAY EXECUTIVE COMMITTEE

Theory was all very well, but practice was another matter. There was an uneasy feeling that the masses might think, as did the despised intellectuals, that the levelling of society under a common strain, the enormously increased production and the community spirit fostered by the war, were a vindication of Socialism. The intellectuals, in spite of the nominal party truce, made much propaganda offering the country a complete Socialist programme of full employment, nationalisation, and an equal-shares-for-all Welfare State. *The Queen* was not slow to scent this threat. There were constant polemics against the Labour Party's 'specious arguments, fallible clichés, promises that cannot be fulfilled, and bitter meagre attacks on the Tories based on unprincipled distortion of the truth'. It was an awkward position. Privilege could not protest against rationing, increased wages for munition workers, state direction of industry, financial controls, for this would be unpatriotic in wartime. But these things, the longer they lasted, were chiselling away at the old order which they were resolved to maintain. 'It is a measure of our determination to win the war that we are willing to tolerate all the regulations without complaint for the duration. But is it going to be a question of the duration only? This is the unpleasant misgiving which each successive Plan for a Brave New World is apt to awake in the observant.' 'It is up to us to keep an increasing vigil lest after the war is over we find that the freedom we thought we had loaned for a common task is not given back to us.'

They raged away at anyone who threatened their position. 'The Labour members of the L.C.C. suggest that public schools give their pupils a good conceit of themselves as more or less predestined leaders, and foster class feelings. It almost looks as if prejudice rather than judgement influences their decisions. If they would look about their comrades they might be enlightened. Mr Attlee was at Haileybury, Mr Dalton and Mr Pethwick Lawrence are both Etonians. Perhaps the L.C.C. labourists would say that these three escaped the class taint and did not acquire the good conceit of themselves as predestined leaders; nevertheless they do lead, and it is Labour they lead isn't it?' 'The B.B.C. still pursue the policy of allowing clergymen, writers and others to discuss the New Order in Europe. Time enough to discuss all this when we have won the war, and you may be pretty certain that the people responsible for the New Order in Europe will not be those gentlemen who are discussing it at present.'

Hopefully, they tried to dismiss the possibility of nationalisation. After the miners' strike: 'The public are not prepared to nationalise

Soon  now!

after five years with the Services

HEINZ
57

will be home with you again

the coal-mines in order to hand them over to men who have struck such a deadly blow to the nation in the great crisis of the war. Nationalisation is dead.' 'Now we come back to Sir William Beveridge. You all remember Sir William don't you? I must call your attention to his scheme because some of you are far too inattentive. After this war the citizen, whatever class he believes himself to grace, will become a servant of the state. His children will be born in state clinics. They will be educated in state kindergartens and state schools. In exchange for your liberty, good people, you will have *security*. Isn't that marvellous? No risk, no trouble.'

Mr Herbert Morrison

Victory came and *The Queen* celebrated it by totting up the number of peers who had lost their lives on active service. Twenty-three it came to, and thirty-one baronets. In addition, five peers had been killed in air raids and two baronets had died while prisoners of war. They noticed that the sons of the Princess Royal had known the hardships of the life of a private soldier, and that commissions were gained from the ranks, but it was plain that most officers were gentlemen, and this vital fact had led to victory perhaps more than any other. The country would doubtless be grateful for it. The Election would give them a chance to prove it. But there was the matter of the Socialists to be dealt with. 'An attempt is being made to change the whole system and way of life of the nation and to convert it into a Socialist State where we shall be marshalled, controlled, directed by officials and dictators. It will be a Britain under the Bureaucrats. It will be no different from Germany under the Nazis. If you want that sort of life you will vote for the Socialists or Communists or Commonwealth candidates. If you prefer to live the life of free men and women you will vote for the National candidate and so support Mr Churchill.'

The Election was lost. *The Queen* expressed astonishment that the public misunderstood what had been done for them. The people who had rallied to Churchill in 1940 elected a Labour Government in 1945. 'England has dropped The Pilot. The world is shocked at her ingratitude to the man whose courage and sagacity, whose leadership, and political and military capacity held the enemy at bay until the United Allies were able to save the world. His was the voice of England.' *The Queen* did not detect a change in that voice, from the early days of the war, a new note in it perhaps of privilege.

In any case, England now had a different voice.

Victory roll

Into the Sixties

Her Majesty rides to Westminster

*Today every man can enjoy
not only security and education and health,
but he can be a snob as well.*

Privilege in its traditional form was dead. The Edwardians had claimed that centuries of power and wealth had perfected the social system of England. 'Let the Socialists rail as they will, our upper classes are the finest body of thinkers and livers in the world.' Now the Socialists had come to power. The resentment of the upper classes was great. Instead of the luxury and comfort which they had looked for after the long drabness of war, even greater restrictions were imposed. Austerity was essential if the Welfare State was to be established at the same time as Britain was struggling to bring about economic recovery. For the first time the upper classes were cut off from the sources of power and influence. In addition, they were poorer and more heavily taxed than they had ever been before: 'Imported pastry cooks in ducal country houses were alas put down when income tax rose to nineteen and six in the pound. At weekends now, therefore, one must be content with biscuits out of a tin. In fact the cost of graceful living has reached what illiterate economists call the ceiling.'

Everything that a reader of *The Queen* might care about seemed to have disappeared forever. 'Were there ever really taxis at midnight in Berkeley Square. Did we read the dinner party menu with care, checking the ever eager butler's renewal of our glass, refusing many dishes? Did we deny ourselves martinis at the day's third cocktail party?'

Princess Anne and Prince Charles

They were no longer able to live in places which they thought suitable: 'While there is doubtless blue blood in Belgravia in 1952 more of it is now to be found in the little mews and lanes in the rear of the great houses than behind Basevi's stuccoed and still impressive façades. Today many of the descendants of the original inhabitants of the area live in the humble purlieus that a hundred years ago housed their forebears' grooms and coachmen. They drink beer on Sunday mornings in the fashionable little pubs that were once patronised by the footmen of the great houses. The war accelerated the change and made it irrevocable. Government offices invaded Belgravia in force between 1939 and 1945, and when the tide of war at last receded the private residents for the most part did not return. A handful of them, notably Mr Henry Channon, M.P., keep alive the residential tradition of Belgrave Square. It is to the little streets—to Kinnerton Street, Wilton Row and Groom Place for example—that much of the residential focus of Belgravia has shifted.'

Even Buckingham Palace was not safe: 'There have been one or two changes at Court since I last wrote. Mr Ernest Popplewell, M.P. for Newcastle, has become Vice-Chamberlain of the Household. This, of course, is a political appointment and it says much for the times in which we live that Mr Popplewell is an ex-railway porter.'

The three Queens,
Queen Elizabeth, the Queen Mother and Queen Mary,
at the funeral of George VI

The Coronation procession,
leaving Buckingham Palace (1953)

Fashion in Tahiti (1960)

Queen Charlotte's Ball (1959)

Ellen, Countess of Dysart, had foreseen thirty or forty years before what would happen. She pointed out that Socialism was 'the veriest tyranny which would fall heaviest on the working classes. The rich would migrate.' Under the Socialist Government many of the rich did just that. 'On all sides one hears news of people leaving the old country in an endeavour to avoid the prevailing austerity and mode of living.' There was a flight of dukes to Africa, and other grandees to the Continent, the Bahamas, to Jersey—to anywhere where taxation would not finally cripple them. England for them was finished. 'A new Aristocracy is beginning to take shape, an aristocracy in which power and privilege seem likely to be shared between the bureaucrat, the expert and the trades union boss.' Those who stayed behind faced a dismal future, one in which even Royalty had to economise. 'The world was delighted when confirmation of the Royal romance rumours at last issued from Buckingham Palace. Princess Elizabeth and Prince Philip of Greece as he then was, having known each other since childhood fell in love in the secluded beauty of the Scottish Highlands when staying last summer at Balmoral. His Majesty who has been so keenly alive to the economic perils of the nation, and who would wish to do nothing to distract the nation from its task of greater production to overcome the crisis, has cordially agreed the sumptuousness and overflowing lavishness of bygone Royal Weddings ought not to be repeated this year.'

Ted Hill, Chairman of the Trades Union Council

The Duke of Edinburgh in New Delhi with President Nehru

The prospect was one of progressive dwindling: 'It is no doubt true that, whether by some form of tax evasion, by the profits on the sale of shares or by deliberate spending of capital, quite a number of people do manage to postpone their descent to the standard of living destined for them in the post war world. But they can only postpone it. Before long the stark new society will take shape, no longer cushioned or disguised by survivals from an earlier more luxurious age.' They tried at times to put a brave face on it. 'The London Season still returns every year, but now belongs entirely to the young to whom the Presentation is as important as it ever was. The young people of today are, I think, infinitely nicer than most of my own generation. They are friendly, kind to older people, honest and absolutely free from snobbishness. The tolerant, generous youths I meet at White's or the St James's are nearly all earning their living at something or other. Good luck to them!' 'I know that the very suggestion of a dinner jacket at a Hunt Ball would make our grand-fathers turn in their graves, but personally I would much rather see young fellows in their dinner jackets than not at all.' At other times they endeavoured rather fruitlessly to recapture some things of their erstwhile privileged attitudes, relying especially upon tradition to bolster them up. 'Our Masters will try to work up an agitation against the House of Lords for electioneering purposes, but the omens do not at the moment look favourable. The Lords did good work in preventing the abolition of capital punishment for murder, and they get full credit for that among the majority of the nation.'

Jazz musicians

This point of view covered almost all affairs. Lord Goddard was highly commended for his rigorous interpretation of his function: 'Speaking of crime, is it not about time there was an enquiry into the Borstal System? The ease with which its inhabitants continue to escape whenever they are so minded almost suggests that imprisonment in Borstal is rather farcical . . . If an enquiry is held let us hope that Lord Goddard is President. No Judge in my recollection has shown more common sense on the Bench and upheld the law better . . . The Court of Appeal was set up to correct wrong verdicts and sentences. Lord Goddard does not encourage frivolous appeals. The other day a man who had got a three year sentence invited Lord Goddard to revise or reduce it. He got six years—just double. This sort of thing is apt to reduce the amount of business going to the Appeal Court.'

Blood sports were defended with passion—those against them being reminded that the fox enjoyed it: 'The movement to attack huntin' shootin' and fishin' gathers strength and should be watched . . . Those who believe in old English honest sportsmanship will do well to look to their interest before it is too late and Parliament is rushed by the same crowd as staged the vote on hanging . . .' 'Two societies which specialise in opposition to "cruel sports" write to inform me that their bill is only aimed at hunting and coursing . . .

It aims to protect the deer, fox, otter, badger, hare and rabbit and it specifies that it does not forbid shooting these animals. What can be more uncertain or cruel than shooting foxes? They would probably prefer sport with the hounds rather than a display with shotguns such as we had in northern counties a few months ago when farmers insisted on putting down foxes, went out with scores of guns, got one or two in a day and sometimes none . . . You may recall that one of Adolf Hitler's first acts was to abolish hunting!'

The Fourth of June at Eton

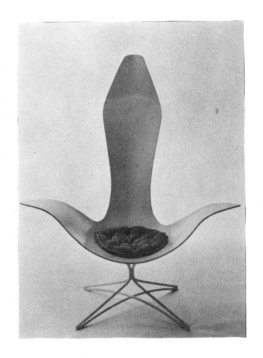

Lord Altrincham was slated for his attack on the Queen: 'Nearly three weeks have passed since Lord Altrincham's circulation-boosting article caught the eye of Fleet Street. The naturally chivalrous instincts of man to woman lead one to the conclusion that it is caddish to insult publicly any woman in whatever walk of life she may be. It is particularly reprehensible to do so to such a diligent and conscientious person as the Queen, who, by the nature of her exalted position, is unable to reply . . . Is he really so unsubtle that he cannot understand how vital *mystique* is to Monarchy? . . .'

Picasso and Graham Sutherland were not yet accepted by those who claimed not to know much about it but to know what they liked. 'Picasso has inflicted his art once again on London, timed so it seems to synchronise with the opening of the Royal Academy. I have not myself seen his pictures, but I am extremely amused by the criticisms I have read so far. It appears that no one, no matter how competent he or she may be, has yet expressed any ability to understand them or what they represent. You can *buy* a painting described in the

Henry Moore with the shadow of his King and Queen

Daily Telegraph as a "contraption resembling a wind direction indicator with a small propellor, surmounting the ghostly cone-shaped head of the woman". It is entitled Femme au Chapeau and is modestly priced at £5000. To turn to something more refreshing and healthy, did you see Pietro Annigoni's paintings? This is real art which even I can understand.'

The decline in standards of behaviour at Ascot was deplored: 'Discipline has declined in the Royal Enclosure at Ascot. I do not deplore the new fashion that women may, unrebuked, go to the rails and make their own bets. Men therefore have less to do. But females now smoke all over the place, *and* the grass is affronted with red-stained cigarette ends. I even saw one girl without a hat, unless she can describe some horse's black noseband as a hat. Years ago such a damsel would have been flung out. I can sympathise with young men who evidently having been too far back in the queue at Moss Bros. had to turn up in bowler hats; but why need they also wear their grandfathers' white spats?'

Sir Laurence Olivier
in the Seagram Building, New York.
The tapestry is by Picasso

THE ESTABLISHMENT CHRONICLE

In the old days we had it quite straight in our minds that Establishment figures were quiet, not flashy; unruffled; unobtrusively powerful; never made mistakes; never complained of one another; never resigned and were proved wrong. In short, they were the top Old Boy Network. However, it has been brought to the notice of the Governing Body that a certain degree of confusion has arisen over the rules of this closely-knit Association. For example, a Mr. Henry Fairlie wrote a rather muddling article in a well-known magazine. Also, one of our brighter boys, Boothby, has been heard to complain that the Association has done him down; Salisbury, whom we used to consider most reliable, has been expelled for misconduct. His excuse is that he didn't understand the rules. Everyone is agreed about Bedford's dismissal, but there are those who feel that if Chandos had been punished at once for setting up his own gang, matters would not have reached such a sorry state of affairs. These grave things and other little ones, like Hailsham bathing at Bournemouth, Eccles wearing those fearful shiny shoes, Gilmour employing Taper, Churchill minor going on too much, Mancroft joining G.U.S., Roxburghe shooting a fox (expulsion is under consideration)—all these have decided the Governing Body to issue a revised set of rules. Members are earnestly requested to peruse and study them carefully for hereafter ignorance of the rules will be no excuse and flouting them will be severely punished (unless a compromise can be reached).

Sycophancy was no longer essential to The Queen in 1959. It could even show disrespect for the Establishment

*Photograph of the members of the Establishment
taken on the occasion of the
Extraordinary Annual General Meeting
held on Commonwealth Day at White's Club.*

Front row:
Left to right: L. Mountbatten, E. Waugh,
J. Rothenstein, J. Wyndham, A. Pryce-Jones,
A. Devonshire, M. Sargent, B. Norfolk.

Second row:
I. Jacob, L. Scarbrough, C. Cobbold,
H. Macmillan, Mr. Canterbury, N. Brook,
J. Astor, F. Hoyer Millar.

Third row:
N. Birkett, E. Heath, J. Wolfenden,
H. Drogheda, C. Boyd-Rochfort, T. Eliot,
D. Kilmuir, W. Cowdray, I. Kirkpatrick,
R. Makins, W. Haley, J. Kemsley,
P. Sinker, D. Hamilton, D. Crawford.

Back row:
O. Dawnay, V. Bonham Carter, W. Monckton,
H. Beaufort, G. Jebb, M. Bowra,
H. Kindersley, R. Birley, C. Radcliffe,
A. Lennox-Boyd, D. Bowes-Lyon, H. Nicolson,
I. Berlin, K. Clark.

The Cambridge Boat Race crew in training

Teenagers (1959)

But it was all no good. Privilege for the aristocracy was over and done with. Their traditions, shorn of the power that went with them, were as meaningless as a troop of Beefeaters—colourful perhaps, but lacking any real importance. But while the formerly privileged classes were trying to re-create a world which no longer existed, England was progressing independently. The year 1951 saw the return of the Conservatives, but it was not a return to rule by privilege. The Election was won as much as anything by the promise of the 300,000 new houses which Mr Macmillan was going to build; and he was going to build them for the working classes. The Tories were embracing policies which would have been dismissed as ludicrous twenty-five years before. Within two years it was possible to write: 'This past year has been remarkable for so many signs of recovery that we may feel our convalescence as a nation is now over. How quickly it has been accomplished.'

Mrs Rose Butler and
Miss Sydney Wade-Gery at
the Chelsea Flower Show

Eton picnic:
Miss Mary McDougall and
Viscount Feilding

*Princess Alexandra
in Nairobi*

The King of Siam

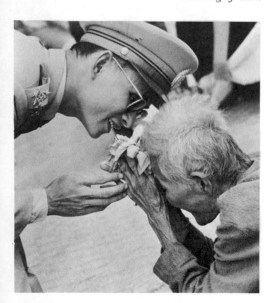

The Queen's *new breadth
of interest was shown in
Henri Cartier-Bresson's photographs
of Red China* (1959)

The change was complete. 'Britain has always had a privileged
class. Today it is the working class. Theirs in this half century is the
power, theirs the glory. In their stately homes—homes provided by
the state—for which they are privileged to pay negligible rents, these
gentry modestly taxed, lead lives of increasing leisure in an environment of increasing ease.' Here was the truth of it. The Welfare State
had been transformed into the Affluent Society. Two things resulted.
First, the conflict between the classes became virtually unnecessary
in the face of standardised living, off-the-peg clothes and popular
culture. Secondly, politics became too vast and unmanageable and
too serious for one small *élite* to cope with. Scientific advances,
countrywide building and education schemes, post-war economics, all
these made Government a highly technical affair. Life henceforward
had to be lived on two levels, first the realistic and secondly the social.
Before it had been possible for social life to have more meaning, for
those who ruled were also those who had the money to entertain and
enjoy themselves. Society without its power was meaningless and
frivolous. And there were more and more people, with money but
without power, anxious to take part in the frivolities.

W. Somerset Maugham

Almost everyone became privileged. Fashions for the first time had come from below—television, teddy-boy clothes, beatnik clothes—these were fads which spread upwards. Society became a game which anyone could play. U non-U, IN or OUT, this was what became important. Now that it was of no consequence, in the sense of power, whether you were in or out—now that you did not have to prove your upper classness by the exercise of influence, everyone could join in—be smart, be one move ahead. 'It is hard work keeping up with being smart because the range of smart conduct keeps changing. Some things are obviously smart because the experts all tell us so. Thus it is now smart to be able to cook Coquille St Jacques, to know what petillant means, to vote Liberal and to live in Wiltshire.' No one could be better at this sort of game than *The Queen*. They did not need Nancy Mitford to teach them how to be snobs. 'I don't really object to snobbery if it is done on the grand scale, but I like a snob to *be* a snob and to demonstrate it in all he says and does. If he can introduce a little subtlety, a touch of the unusual into his approach, so much the better.' Nor did they need Mr Evelyn Waugh to quote Lord Curzon that no gentleman has soup at luncheon.

Gilbert Harding

The Queen could complicate the game so that only about five hundred people could play it with any confidence: 'There are two kinds of people and two kinds of things in this world: IN and OUT. A thing can be IN for three reasons, (a) because it is so classic and great, (b) because it is so obscure, (c) because it is so far OUT even the OUT people won't touch it for example Tchaikovsky. Everything that is not IN is OUT. OUT people can never be IN. Really IN people can't be OUT no matter what they do, but an IN person who works at being IN is automatically OUT.' The status symbols they also knew about, advising on the smartness of keeping lavatory paper on a plate weighed down with a stone. They enjoyed the money boom: 'When did you last hear the word austerity. At this minute there is more money in Britain than ever before. Nearly two thousand million pounds, is pouring out of pockets and wallets and handbags (the gold mesh one pictured above costs 5 gns from Jarrolds) and changing into air tickets and oysters, television sets and caviar, art treasures and vacuum cleaners, cigars and refrigerators. . . . Britain has launched into an era of unparalleled lavish living. It came unobtrusively. But now you are living in a new world.'

Marilyn Monroe and Arthur Miller

Albert Finney

*Mr Felix Fenston, one of
the post-war property millionaires*

It was indeed a new world. Luckily it was one in which it was smart to take a more liberal view—smart to care about the bomb, smart to like good books and plays. 'Much ado about Nottingham, much ado about Notting Hill and Notting Dale and suddenly everybody is discussing the so-called "colour problem".' In 1957 it was possible to ask the Earl of Birkenhead to write a tribute to Sir Anthony Eden: 'This country has long been in the habit of congratulating itself upon its traditional love of fair play, and its magnanimity in the face of a stricken opponent. These laurels are now sadly withered in the venomous hatred with which Eden's opponents poisoned the closing stages of his political life, achieving at last the *moment d'extase* by his fall, in the buoyant hulloos of exultation whooping like primeval war-cries from telephone to telephone, crowing over his fall, quoting the latest Osbert Lancaster, and indecently questioning his sickness . . . Who was not first conscious of excitement, indeed of pride, when they heard that the British were going back to that Suez which so many of them thought they should never have left?' By 1961 such a view would not be tenable.

The Royal Tour of India (1961)

Mr Antony Armstrong-Jones was married to Princess Margaret. Even the Crown had accepted the transfer of privilege to other hands. It was a far cry from the days when Queen Victoria insisted on seeing the proofs of each copy of *The Queen*.

The Queen
fortnightly

DATE DUE

DEC 2 1 1984 OCT 30 84			
201-6503		Printed in USA

rs of Privilege

il must, of course, be left to individual taste. The four ribbon ...are from 14 to 16 inches long, which are turned in at the ...om to form a point, the ribbon being embroidered or not at ...sure. The little articles forming pendants to them are made in ...following manner:—

The little Needlebook. For this purpose fold a piece of card-...d, line it with white silk, and cover with some of the ribbon; ...half of the needlebook must, of course, be the same breadth ...he ribbon. Then fasten two leaves of fine white flannel inside, ...hed round the edges, and secure the whole by an elastic band, ...which it must be attached to the pointed end of the ribbon.

The little bag, a receptacle for the thimble, reels of cotton, &c., is likewise made of two pieces of the ribbon joined together, ...a narrow runner made under the frill at the top, through ...ch a fine silk cord is passed to draw and undraw the bag. It ...ld be about 3 inches long, and fastened on one side underneath ...frill to the ribbon.

The pincushion is made of two round pieces of cardboard, ...red with the ribbon, and sewn together, the pins being stuck ...he seam to form a decoration for the outer edge.

.The scissors are merely hung on to a piece of elastic, which is ...ened to the point of the ribbon. The four pieces of ribbon ...uld be united at the top and finished off by a rosette made of six ...rs and three ends, arranged in a circle on a net foundation. ...h of the bows and ends requires about 3½ inches of ribbon, ...des a small piece to complete the centre of the rosette. On the ...ng side of this rosette a common dress-hook of rather a large ...should be sewn, by which means the necessaire is attached to ...waistband.

6. PETTICOAT INSERTION.

...an explanation of this pattern is scarcely necessary, the differ-...e between the open and thick embroidery being so very plainly ...wn in our illustration. The holes should be cut out and sewn ...r, whilst the remainder of the pattern should be executed in ...l raised satin stitch and button-hole stitch, taking care to trace ...well, to give the pattern a raised appearance when finished. The ...poses for which this insertion may be used besides for petticoats ...very numerous, as it is suitable for letting in round the bottom ...a child's frock, as also for ornamenting the skirt of a lady's ...rning dress, made in any kind of white material.

...'. "L. C." with coronet for the corner of a pocket-handkerchief.

8. BOW FOR A CRAVAT OR NECK-TIE.

Materials: 1½ yard of a good lilac sarsnet ribbon, about 4 inches ...de, 2 skeins of fine white purse silk, small black beads of two ...ferent sizes, a small piece of good black silk net.

...We have given an illustration of an embroidered cravat or neck-... and also a wristlet to match, as we think our readers may like ...try and make a set of these useful little appendages to the toilet. ...ey are extremely fashionable, and may be made in any colour, ...t should correspond generally with the dress that they are to ...company. To make this bow, the rich pattern shown in our ...graving should first be drawn on both ends of the ribbon, and a ...ce of black silk net laid under it. The work should now be ...ked on to a piece of toile cirée, or stiff paper, and the pattern, ...embroidered in chain-stitch with the white silk. The outer edge ...the pattern should be worked in button-hole stitch, to make it ...ong and firm when cut out. After the embroidery is finished, ...e ribbon should be cut away in the places indicated in our ...ttern, and the black beads sewn on, the effect of the net-ground ...ing extremely light and pretty. When both ends are embroi-...red, the ribbon should be made up into a nicely arranged bow.

9. WRISTLETS TO MATCH THE NECK-TIE.

Materials: 2½ yards of lilac sarsnet ribbon 3 inches wide, some ...od black silk net, 2 skeins of fine white purse silk, black beads of ...o different sizes, lining, &c.

The wristlet, should, of course, be made in exactly the same ...loured ribbon as the neck-tie, and embroidered to correspond. ...e wristlet itself is very simple, and is nearly covered by the bow ...aced on the top of it. To make it, take about 12 inches of the ...bbon, and line it with a piece of thin white silk or ribbon, about ...inch wide, put on at an equal distance from both edges, and run ...ouble on each side for a piece of elastic to be put through. The ...ning should be so arranged that the ribbon has a puffed appear-...ce in the middle, and after the elastic is run through it should be ...stened to the side of the wrist. To make the bow, take 23 inches ...the ribbon, and draw the large pattern on one end of it and the ...aller one on the other, in the same way as shown in our engraving. ...he ends should be embroidered in the same manner as those of the ...ck-tie, with black net, white silk, and black beads, which it will ...t be necessary to describe again. The ribbon should now be made ...p into a bow with one end longer than the other, as shown in our ...graving, and the bow fastened on to the seam of the wristlet. ...f course the long end of the ribbon should fall on the outside.

THE FASHIONS.

MANY of our readers are, no doubt, acquainted with a volume ...ublished in France at the beginning of this century, called ...The English in Paris." It was ornamented with a number ...f woodcuts, which most expressively illustrated our fathers' and ...others' mode of dressing. Evidently our susceptible neighbours ...ere not wholly inclined to applaud the poke bonnets of our women ...r the broad-brimmed hats of our men. For many years we were ...xposed to the ridicule of our fastidious friends the French, on the ...core of the very inelegant costumes which were the work of our ...ressmakers and milliners. *Nous avons changé tout cela.* To any ...rdinary, or extraordinary, observer's eye, it is clear that an English-...woman of position and taste dresses, at the present moment, as well ...s the most approved *Parisienne.* Whether in country or in town, at ...the family mansion or the sea-side, on the continent or at an English ...watering-place—whether walking, riding, driving, dancing, boating,

Design," and to have benefited by the instruction. And is it not a good thing to dress well?—whatever is worth doing at all, is worth doing well. Should we not, then, attire our body in the most suitable, most appropriate, and most "taking" costume? We are certainly in opinion that we should; and, being so, shall, from time to time, in the pages of THE QUEEN, describe the newest, the prettiest, and the latest *modes* both in Paris and in London, so that our readers may know, upon the very best authority, all the changes that take place in that important part of the world of Fashion, with which we have here to do.

As at this time of the year nearly everybody is travelling or staying at the sea-side, and as the weather is still exceedingly warm, little attention is being paid to toilets suitable for the coming season. In consequence of there being so few people in town, novelties have not as yet appeared in our first West-end houses, but these, we are told, are in the course of preparation, and soon we hope to initiate our readers into the mysteries of mantles, cloaks, bonnets, dresses, &c., for the coming winter, and so give them some idea of what are likely to be the prettiest and most fashionable garments, with the mode of making them.

DRESSES, which we will commence with, as being one of the most important articles of a lady's toilet, are being worn in grenadine, barège, and light silks, for occasions when rather a dressy toilet is required. For morning wear, dresses of white piqué, braided in black poil de chèvre, mohair, and articles of that description, seem to be in favour, the latter materials being very suitable for the cool fresh mornings of September. Grenadine dresses are very prettily made with three quilled or fluted flounces at the bottom of the skirt, these flounces being bound with a narrow sarsnet ribbon, and having a heading at the top, also bound with ribbon. Two of these flounces are sometimes carried on each side up the front of the skirt, leaving the bottom one to go all round. We will give the description of another pretty grenadine dress which we noticed at a very good dressmaker's. It was of a very light grey, figured with cerise sprigs, and was made with five narrow flounces at the bottom of the skirt bound with cerise ribbon. The sash was made of grenadine bound with the same ribbon, and was fastened by a large bow on the left side.

We also remarked a plain grey silk dress, trimmed at the bottom of the skirt with a crossway piece of black silk about nine inches in depth, stitched on with bright orange silk; the dress was made with a Zouave jacket, trimmed with a band of crossway black silk stitched on with orange, and the jacket was fastened in front by four black-and-orange buttons. Any plain coloured silk dress would look prettily made in this manner, either bright blue, green, or lilac; but, in this case, stitching the black silk on with the same colour as that of the dress; we noticed a bright Napoleon blue dress trimmed with three rows of handsome black guipure insertion, placed at intervals on the skirt, and a blue ruche on each side of the insertions. The body, which was open in front and made with points (for these appear to be coming into favour), was trimmed with blue ruches and black lace, as were also the sleeves. A black silk dress suitable for mourning, was ornamented with a broad jet trimming, put on round the bottom of the skirt in the form of an 8; the trimming was also carried up the front of the skirt *en tablier.*

Lace mantles and shawls seem to be in as great favour as ever for midday walks and rides; but now the evenings are getting cool, these garments must, of course, be exchanged for something warmer. The black embroidered cachemire shawls and the large burnous in thin light cloth are among the most suitable articles for evening wear out of doors. Indian cachemire shawls, which are at all times elegant and recherché, can never be substituted by anything so suitable for wearing between the seasons. They are manufactured in such gorgeous colours and in such exquisite designs, and, besides, are so durable, that one of these shawls may be considered as the most elegant and useful article of a lady's toilet. We have seen some very pretty white grenadine cloaks, some lined with a pale-coloured silk, others merely bound with black velvet, and others trimmed with broad lace and black velvet, the latter being extremely elegant. For mourning, shawls and burnous of black grenadine, and trimmed with a crossway band of black silk, are very simple and in excellent taste.

Just now, crinoline bonnets are in favour, being worn both in black and white. We noticed a very pretty black one trimmed on the left side with a bunch of yellow roses mixed with black lace, and another black one almost covered with white roses and black rosettes mixed with steel ornaments, which are now very much used in the manufacture of black flowers. Black ribbon is also in great favour for trimming all kinds of bonnets, whether straw, crape, or crinoline; mixed with bunches of artificial field flowers or fruit, it has a very stylish effect. A white crape bonnet which struck us as being rather pretty had a drawn front in black silk, the curtain of white crape was covered with a deep row of black lace, and on the left side of the bonnet, placed rather high, was a large bunch of purple grapes, mingled with black lace and green leaves. The bandeau consisted of a black velvet plait with a bunch of grapes on one side.

Muslin bodies, made in every variety of shape and style appear to be more worn than ever. They are excessively convenient and comfortable for the warm weather, and are particularly suitable for a dinner toilet, when a low dress is not required. For wearing under Zouave jackets, we have noticed some pretty little novelties in the way of chemisettes, with collars and cuffs embroidered in black or red, and some trimmed with black lace and velvet. These chemisettes we have also seen in foulard and cachemire, and are extremely stylish worn as a full body without the Zouave jacket. A foulard chemisette, of a pale grey colour, was made with full bishop sleeves and turned-back cuffs embroidered in lilac, with a collar embroidered to correspond; another of bright mauve spotted with white was made in the same manner, but with plain wristbands. With the latter, plain linen cuffs and collars should be worn. These useful little articles are extremely stylish made in cachemire, particularly those in white embroidered in black and trimmed with black velvet.

Head-dresses are now being made generally with a mixture of lace and velvet, except for full dress, when wreaths are generally worn, made of flowers to match those with which the dress is trimmed. The following are some of the newest we have seen, the style

composed of five narrow rolls of scarlet velvet, plaited to form a coronet and mounted on wire pointed in front. Two straps of the same coloured velvet were placed over the plait on the left side, whilst a long white ostrich-feather fastened in with a steel ornament finished off the right side of the head-dress. The feather was exceedingly long, to droop on the shoulder. Another was composed of blue velvet and blue ribbon, both of the same shade, and both three inches wide. These were twisted lightly together, and fe... ... ornamented ... whole finished ... these ends were ... coronet for a ... by buds and ... roses mingled ... the head-dress ... flowers for ... pointed and ...ecting the front and back of the head-dress. In wearing a wreath of this description, the hair should be dressed in loops on each side, and the spray of flowers would entirely conceal the parting of the hair behind. A bridal wreath made in this manner was extremely pretty, very long and very wide tulle lappets being fastened under this long spray, and falling down on either side.

THE SUPPLEMENTS.

THE TOILETS IN THE COLOURED PLATE.

WALKING-DRESS.—The straw bonnet on the left-hand figure is trimmed with black lace, field flowers, and cerise ribbon, arranged in the following manner:—The front of the bonnet is bound with ribbon, the bandeau inside is composed of flowers, and the cap on each side consists of a quilling of black blonde at the top, and white blonde at the bottom. The top of the bonnet is trimmed outside with a half wreath of flowers and foliage, with a piece of broad black lace falling towards the crown. The curtain is made of tulle, over stiff black net, is bound with cerise ribbon, and finished off by a row of broad black lace. The dress is made of brown silk, and is trimmed with the same material, but of a darker shade. A piece of the dark silk forms a graduated trimming up the front of the body and skirt, this trimming being 2½ inches at the neck and at the bottom of the skirt, and only 1½ inches wide at the waist, and is ornamented with large silk buttons. The bottom of the skirt is trimmed all round with a piece of dark brown silk, 5 inches deep, put on with a cording to make a finish, at the top; the silk forming the trimming up the skirt is also corded on both sides. The sleeve is rather large, and is trimmed with the same dark silk, 2½ inches wide, which trimming is carried on the upper part of the sleeve up to the armhole, where it is stitched in with the sleeve. Besides the broad silk trimming, the front of the body and skirt are also ornamented with straps of narrow sarsnet ribbon ¾ inch wide, arranged in various lengths. The length of the longest piece of ribbon at the bottom of the skirt is 15 inches, the next piece is 12 inches, and the next 9 inches; then again a longer piece of 11 inches, and so on, always diminishing towards the waist. This same trimming is also continued up the front of the body, the ribbons being short at the waist, and lengthening as they approach the top. Ribbons of various lengths are also placed on the sleeve.

YOUNG LADIES' TOILET.—The hair is very simply dressed, being frizzed and arranged in a négligé kind of manner, a bow of bright blue ribbon, to match the trimming on the dress, being placed quite in the centre of the front parting. The dress is made of grey grenadine, of a very delicate shade, and is trimmed with bright blue sarsnet ribbon.

It is made with a full body cut square at the top à la Raphaël, and is gathered in to a band at the waist. A plain piece of grenadine forms the square into which the fulness of the body is gathered at the top, and the square piece is 2½ inches deep in the front. It is trimmed with two rows of ribbon put on plain, and only run on the upper edge to give it more play. A grenadine sash lined with muslin is worn with this dress, the ends of which are trimmed on one side with a quilling of the blue ribbon, whilst on the bows it is put on quite plain. The bishop sleeve, which is very full, particularly at the bottom, is gathered in to a waistband; it has a puff of grenadine at the top, stitched in to the armhole of the dress, and the sleeve is ornamented with five rows of ribbon run on one side only. The wristband has also two rows of ribbon run on it quite plain. There are 8 rows of ribbon on the skirt, all put on at equal distances, and these also are run only on one side of the ribbon. The bottom of the skirt is finished off by a gauffered flounce, 5 inches deep, the top of which is covered by the first row of ribbon, so concealing the part where the flounce is put on. A piece of lace is tacked round the square body, whilst a piece of narrow velvet, with a bow in the centre, should be worn round the neck to make a pretty finish to the toilet.

THE PHOTOGRAPH OF HER MAJESTY.

CASTING our eyes backward but a little from the present year, we shall find that Photography existed only for a few. There were not many artists, and those artists had not the means of producing a great number of portraits. Gradually, with photographic printing as with all other printing, the number of artists, together with the means of production, increased; and a reduction in price of course followed. Artistic photography, however, is still comparatively rare, and we have to congratulate the public, Mr. Mayall, and ourselves, on the success of this first attempt—declared by many to be a daring attempt—to give to the public with a printed journal a photographic portrait. We shall, from time to time, issue with this paper photographic portraits of men and women distinguished by station, beauty, talent, or moral worth; but it was thought that nothing could be more appropriate, to begin with, than a Portrait of our beloved Sovereign Lady; and we trust that the success which has accompanied the attempt may prove a happy omen for the career of

"THE QUEEN."